ᴜs

DO NOT REMOVE
CARDS FROM POCKET

Policy Choices

FRAMING THE DEBATE FOR MICHIGAN'S FUTURE

Policy Choices

FRAMING THE DEBATE FOR MICHIGAN'S FUTURE

Edited by

Timothy S. Bynum
Joel Cutcher-Gershenfeld
Phyllis T. H. Grummon
Brendan P. Mullan
Karen Roberts
and
Carol S. Weissert

Michigan State University Press
East Lansing
1993

Copyright © 1993 Institute for Public Policy and Social Research

All Michigan State University Press books are produced on paper which meets the requirements of American National Standard of Information Sciences— Permanence of paper for printed materials ANSI Z23.48-1984.

Michigan State University Press
East Lansing, Michigan 48823-5202

Printed in the United States of America

01 00 99 98 97 96 95 94 93 1 2 3 4 5 6 7 8 9 10

Library of Congress Cataloging-in-Publication Data

Policy choices : framing the debate for Michigan's future / edited by S. Timothy S. Bynum . . . [et al.]
    p.   cm.
Includes bibliographical references and index.
  ISBN 0-87013-344-6
  1. Michigan—Economic Policy. 2. Education and State—Michigan. 3. Medical Policy—Michigan. I. Bynum, Timothy S.
HC107.M5P65 1993
330.9774—dc20
                                      93-31939
                                        CIP

Published with the support of the Institute for Public Policy and Social Research, Michigan State University

Acknowledgements

The Editorial Board was assisted in its efforts by Dr. Joanne Basta of the Institute for Public Policy and Social Research. She not only read and edited drafts of the book, but also provided invaluable assistance in coordinating our efforts. We would also like to thank Dr. Jack H. Knott, Director, for conceiving of the idea of a volume on policy issues, giving us the opportunity to work on it, and for supporting its publication.

Timothy S. Bynum
    Associate Director, IPPSR
    Professor, Criminal Justice

Joel Cutcher-Gershenfeld
    Assistant Professor, School of Industrial and Labor Relations

Phyllis T. H. Grummon
    Assistant Professor, Institute for Public Policy and
    Social Research

Brendan P. Mullan
    Assistant Professor, Sociology

Karen Roberts
    Assistant Professor, School of Industrial and Labor Relations

Carol S. Weissert
    Assistant Professor, Political Science

Contents

IV. EDUCATION POLICY

V. HEALTH POLICY IN MICHIGAN

Introduction

In a democracy, our lives are governed by public policy decisions. How much money we have to spend, what services are available to us, how we educate our children; these and many other decisions are determined by the laws enacted by legislatures and the rules and regulations developed by policymakers. As we look to the past and the future, it's clear that policy decisions have become more complex and more significant. Daily, the media covers stories about health care, welfare reform, and crime that have policy implications. Whether they realize it or not, the public is constantly involved in learning about and influencing policy decisions.

In an effort to inform the debates on areas of significant policy interest to Michigan, the Institute for Public Policy and Social Research (IPPSR) at Michigan State University has created an annual volume dedicated to discussion of these issues. This is the first volume in the series. We hope, over time, to contribute an important perspective to policy discussions at all levels of government and among the citizenry. The authors of this volume were asked to help frame these deliberations by discussing the background of the issue, perspectives on the issue from Michigan's experience and those of others nationally, and the key policy options relevant for debate. We did not ask them to reach any conclusions, but rather, to present research and experience which would help decision makers frame the debate and enlighten discussions around policy formation.

The editorial board chose five policy areas for this volume. The volume begins with an overview of Michigan's demographics and how they affect policy. Subsequent sections consider issues related to employment policy, including worker training and workers' compensation. Economic issues and urban policy are discussed in the third section, with a specific focus on distressed communities and the realities facing our black population. Under education policy we consider issues related to assessment and school finance. We close with a section discussing health policy in Michigan.

In the first section, a picture of Michigan is portrayed from several policy vantage points. Brendan Mullan, in "Who is Michigan? A Demographic Analysis" applies the most recent census data to give a demographic overview of the Michigan population. Michigan, as a major industrialized state, mirrors the United States' demographic pattern of having low fertility and mortality levels, and volatile migration flows. However, much more variation in the patterns emerge when his analysis centers on the county, city, and township levels. Through this analysis of Michigan at the smaller geographical regions and lower governmental localities, Mullan aptly identifies the key population policy questions facing Michigan as it prepares to enter the twenty-first century.

Findings from the Michigan Public Policy Survey (MIPPS) conducted in 1992 are presented in the second paper entitled, "What Michigan Thinks: Findings from the Michigan Public Policy Survey." The findings present Michigan citizens' perceptions on a range of topics with policy relevance such as child care, abortion, and the past presidential race. Citizen perceptions of the areas of greatest need for services were also assessed, and are discussed with reference to their policy implications.

In the final article of section one, we move from a broad overview of Michigan demographics, to focusing on a specific Michigan population—African Americans. Nan Johnson's and Bruce Christenson's title best illustrates the thrust of this article: "Racial Differences in Mortality in Michigan: Are African Americans Better Off Now Than in 1960?" Unfortunately, the answer to this question, according to the authors' analysis, is no. In Michigan, the level of mortality for the African American population is higher than the white population, and there is a growing difference between African Americans and whites in expected length of life. Johnson and Christenson not only present the results of their analysis clearly, but they also examine the various factors that contribute to these disturbing statistics.

Section two explores Michigan employment policy. The article on worker training in Michigan delves into the complex array of state and federal job training programs and policies. Joel Cutcher-Gershenfeld and Kevin Ford identify the central issues that impede the process of implementing a comprehensive and effective job training policy for Michigan, such as the concurrent centralization and fragmentation of programs and the politicization of training programs. Their analysis is thoughtful and insightful, and the questions they pose for policymakers about the future course of job training help to lift the thinking above the confusion and politics associated with this issue. In "Workers Compensation in Michigan: A Disabled Disability System?" Karen Roberts identifies the central problems confronting workers' compensation as arising from the conflict between the changing nature of work and the changing nature of workplace injury (e.g., from short-term to long-term injuries, ambiguous causes). The central thesis of her paper considers whether the original bargain struck between employers and workers early in this century is resilient enough to adapt successfully to the workplace demands of today.

Michigan's economic issues and urban policy are addressed in section three. In the first article of this section on the future of distressed communities, Rex LaMore appeals to policymakers, especially at the local level, to build local institutions that are responsive to the needs of low-income residents. He outlines a need for a long-term comprehensive commitment both at state and local levels to address the seemingly intractable economic problems of distressed communities in Michigan. The second article in this section, on the state of black Michigan, complements LaMore's article well, since a disproportionate number of Michigan's black citizens live in these distressed communities. Joe Darden presents a disturbing picture of Michigan moving toward two separate and unequal societies. The inequality is due primarily to persistent racial discrimination, uneven economic investment, and structural changes in the State's economy. While Darden's analysis is disturbing, he also proposes policies for addressing these injustices that should be urgently considered.

The first article in section four on education policy entitled "Assessing Educational Outcomes: Trends and Opportunities," looks at the issues related to standard setting in the school system and the assessment of those standards. The legislature has been clear about the desirability of focusing on outcomes through its passage of Public

Act 25. Less clear has been the best route for assessing those outcomes. In this paper, Phyllis Grummon considers the two most prominent initiatives—proficiency tests and portfolios—as options being pursued in Michigan.

In the last article of this section, we move from assessing educational outcomes to the realm of school financing. In "School Finance: Finding the Dollars to Make Educational Sense" Ruth Beier succinctly describes Michigan's current school financing system, and the problems associated with it (e.g., high property taxes) that have become more acute and controversial in recent years. In the final section of her paper, she discusses the arguments, pro and con, for the three recently debated strategies designed to address the problem of high property taxes and school financing.

The final section of this book ends with a discussion of health care reform in Michigan. Michigan, as the rest of the nation, faces a health care crisis. The state's ability to finance the cost of health care is limited by the slow growth in earnings of much of its working population. Should Michigan act now on reforming its health care, when the Clinton administration and Congress is geared up to address this very issue? Carol Weissert, Andrew Hogan, and Leonard Fleck help to address this question and others by carefully untangling the complexity of factors that contribute to this crisis, and by presenting sane and practical recommendations that policymakers might consider.

I.
Michigan:
A Demographic Overview

Who Is Michigan?
A Demographic Analysis

Brendan Mullan

STATEMENT OF THE PROBLEM

Social and economic problems often have their causes rooted in levels, patterns and trends of population growth, population distribution, and overall population change. Regulation and manipulation of these population levels, patterns, and trends provides a mechanism through which county, state, and federal planners and officials can address related social and economic difficulties and dilemmas. In its most formal definition a "population policy" is defined as a policy "explicitly adopted by governments for [its] presumed demographic consequences."[1] Population policies attempt to modify or transform the "normal" patterns of population growth and composition with the intention that this demographic manipulation will achieve the primary goals of improved economic and social welfare and national/regional security.

At the state level in the United States, the collection, analysis, and transmission of population policy *data* is most often dependent on census data and vital registration statistics to provide information to all levels of government and to relevant private groups and institutions involved in the policymaking arena. One purpose of this chapter is to examine how Michigan's existing population policy experience has been analyzed and how widely the analysis has been disseminated and implemented. A second purpose is to state the key population policy questions facing Michigan as it prepares to enter the next millennium. These key population policy issues can be best understood when they are placed within the context of Michigan's current and recent historical demographic profile; the development of such a demographic profile constitutes the third element of this chapter. Only then can population policy options and the associated relevant research be presented as realistic proposals—proposals that can be compared with the experience of other states and industrialized nations.

Like all industrialized nations, the United States has a broad demographic pattern of low fertility levels, low mortality levels, and extremely volatile migration flows. Michigan is perhaps the epitome of an industrialized state within an industrial economy and, as such, its demographic experiences have mirrored the broader trends. Despite this seeming uniformity of demographic change, Michigan has experienced significant differences and variation in all three key demographic indicators at the county, city, township and lower levels. Michigan is witnessing an upheaval in its demographic map because demographic change does not occur at the same rate or at the same time within or between all geographic divisions. The changes in the demographic weight of different counties, for example, will result inevitably in a changed distribution of economic, social and political priorities, problems, and proposed policy options. Furthermore, the differences in population growth and composition rates at the county level or between north, south, east, and west Michigan will change relations among counties and between regions.

KEY POLICY QUESTIONS

Some of the most salient demographic characteristics of Michigan today are:

- A rapidly changing age composition. The most rapidly growing segment of the population is that over age 65; this is especially true for the white and black populations.
- Women make up the largest part of this growing elderly population.
- The "baby boom" generation, those born between 1946 and the early 1960s, are now in their prime working years.

- Fertility levels remain significantly below the replacement level of 2.1 births per woman.
- Between 1980 and 1990, Michigan experienced a net out-migration of 6.33 percent. There are dramatic county-level differences in migration levels and patterns.
- The racial breakdown of Michigan's population in 1990 was 0.6 percent American Indian, Eskimo, or Aleut; 1.1 percent Asian or Pacific Islander, 2.2 percent Hispanic origin (of any race); 13.9 percent black; and 82 percent white.
- In 1990, 64.1 percent of persons aged 16 and over were in the labor force; for males the figure was 73.4 percent, and for females 55.7 percent. These figures are substantially larger than the comparable figures for 1970 and 1980 because of increased female labor force participation (accompanied by a slight decrease in male labor force participation rates).
- In 1990, 57.1 percent of mothers with children under 6 were in the labor force compared to 41.6 percent in 1980. For mothers with children aged between 6 and 17, the labor force participation rate was 73.3 percent compared to just under 60 percent in 1980.
- The poverty rate for people and households in Michigan has increased significantly in the 1980s. Of those of children under the age of 18, 18.2 percent were estimated as being below the poverty line, while the poverty rate for those over 65 has declined slightly. The number of families in poverty has increased by about 27 percent. In female family households with no spouse present, the poverty rate in 1989 was 35.8 percent.[2] The figures for the city of Detroit are startling; 20.1 percent of the elderly and 46.4 percent of the young were classified as poor.[3]

These broadest of trends give some indication of the key demographic policy questions that Michigan faces:

- The demographic trends of the continued aging of the population and the baby boom generation's eventual retirement may depress growth as savings rates begin to fall. With relatively few old people now, the burden of social security taxes has been light. This will change as the age composition of Michigan tilts toward the aged extreme in the coming decades. In the next 20 years, the ratio of retired people to working people will rise; there will be fewer workers, less capital saving, and perhaps restrained growth just when it is most needed to meet the increased pensions and health costs of an older population.

- Tax increases to pay for state pensions, which today's workers anticipate could dampen economic growth and incentive and reduce the tax base. Private pension schemes will be limited by the decreased flow of savings into equity and bond markets, and the resulting pressure to increase interest rates will threaten economic growth. One critical policy question is what preparations should be encouraged for retirement.
- The aging of Michigan's population presents health-related policy questions in addition to socioeconomic questions. Levels of health care utilization differ significantly according to age, sex, and other subgroupings. High health service utilization rates among those over age 60 are clearly important from a public policy perspective, especially in relation to the increased stresses that will be placed on Medicaid. The process of demographic aging is well established and is projected to continue and intensify. Many of the people who survive to these older ages will have specific types of health care requirements, visual and hearing problems, difficulties related to physical movement and/or communication (both personal and social); long-term health care provision will become a policy priority. In particular, policymakers should pay particular attention to the elderly female population, which is growing faster than the elderly male population. Related to these questions is the notion of the demography of disability that poses such novel policy questions as fertility and mortality decline and the population continues to age.[4]
- The industrialized counties in southern Michigan will continue to experience net out-migration. Those counties in the northern Lower Peninsula with leisure/recreation as the major economic activity will continue to receive significant in-migration. The counties of the Upper Peninsula will continue to have a mixed pattern of migration with in-migration related to return migrants and retirees and out-migration caused by the continuing decline of the industrial/employment base.
- Increased female labor force participation poses obvious policy-related questions in the areas of child-care provision, job-related family leave issues, and occupational restructuring in general. The United States has the highest divorce rate in the industrial world which, when combined with the escalating trend in out-of-wedlock births, means an increase in one-parent families (over 25 percent of all families in the United States are one-parent families) with grave ramifications for household poverty rates.

CHANGE IN MICHIGAN'S POPULATION

Population change is caused by changes in mortality, fertility, and migration. Some of the major changes in these three components of population change in Michigan between 1980 and 1990 are:

- The total population increased by 33,253 people, which represents an increase of less than one-half of 1 percent.
- There were 619,888 more births than deaths—a 6.69 percent increase.
- Net migration was negative, with a net 586,635 people leaving the state.

Thus, Michigan's population, like many populations in industrialized countries, is growing very slowly. Little comfort can be derived from this because populations of individual counties in Michigan have changed dramatically between 1980 and 1990.

Figure 1 is a map of Michigan showing the total population change for the counties of Michigan between 1980 and 1990. The following features are apparent from this map:

- Three (or 20 percent) of the counties in the Upper Peninsula (Chippewa, Mackinac, and Dickinson) gained population.
- The greatest percentage increases in population occurred in Michigan's northern counties (especially Otsego, Montmorency, Crawford, Kalkaska, Grand Traverse, and Leelanau counties). However, these high rates of population change translate into relatively small increases in absolute numbers.
- Wayne county, the state's most populous county, with 2.11 million people in 1990, decreased by 9.67 percent between 1980 and 1990.
- Overall, the southeastern-most counties of the state will continue to grow slowly, with some county declines being offset by others' gains. In absolute numbers of people, however, this slow growth will represent significant increases.

These broad overall trends mask population changes within individual counties and at different ages—changes that often differ dramatically from the aggregate figures.

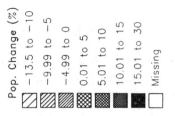

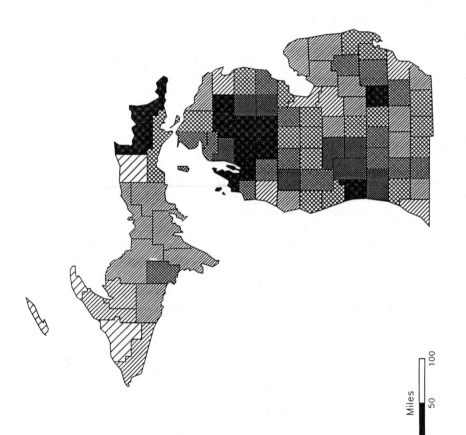

Figure 1. Total Population Changes in Michigan

THE AGE STRUCTURE OF THE POPULATION IN MICHIGAN

The population of Michigan is growing older. In 1990 almost 12 percent of the total population was older than 65, a significant increase from the less than 10 percent of 1980. The change in the proportion of the population over age 65 has been most striking among the female population; almost 14 percent of the female population in Michigan is aged 65 and over. Although the proportion of the black female population at the older ages is less than 10 percent in 1990, the increase from 1980 is as equally striking as that of the overall population. The Hispanic population in Michigan has a dramatically lower proportion at the older ages—in 1990—and a correspondingly higher proportion under age 15. However, with the exception of the Hispanic population, Michigan's population under age 15 has been declining—a trend which will continue well into the twenty-first century.

Some areas of Michigan will experience age distribution distortions more severely than others; in the Upper Peninsula currently just over 19 percent of the female population and 13.5 percent of the male population is over age 65. Contrast these figures with the average of 11 percent of populations over age 65 in the industrialized countries of the world. Already, parts of Michigan have elderly dependency ratios far exceeding the long-range forecasts of 17 percent made for the industrial countries.

The distribution of Michigan's population by broad age groups (under 18, 18 to 64, and 65 and over), for the major racial categories (white, black, and other) for 1990 is shown in table 1, together with the percentage change in size for each group from 1980. For the black and white, the racial categories, the percentage of the population over age 65, both male and female, is notable both in terms of magnitude and, especially, in terms of the significant growth since 1980. White females over the age of 65 have increased in size by just over 21 percent and white males of the same age by just over 18.5 percent since 1980. Striking as these changes are, they are exceeded by the changes in the elderly population of the "others" and blacks. The change in the elderly population classified as "other" reflects the unique demographic characteristics of the Asian, Native American and, especially, the Hispanic populations in Michigan. The significant percentage increase at the older ages for this other population category is tempered somewhat by relatively small absolute numbers underlying the percentage change. Of interest in this third popula-

Table 1.

Michigan's Age Distribution, 1990

White

	Male	% Change from 1980	Female	% Change from 1980
Age 0-18	26.47%	-12.84%	23.90%	-13.06%
Age 18-64	63.04%	0.83%	61.25%	-0.41%
Age 65+	10.49%	18.57%	14.85%	21.03%
Total	100.00%		100.00%	
Population	3,785,843	-1.70%	3,970,243	-1.25%

Black

	Male	% Change from 1980	Female	% Change from 1980
Age 0-18	35.06%	-3.56%	30.18%	-4.16%
Age 18-64	57.38%	10.08%	60.13%	16.09%
Age 65+	7.56%	29.15%	9.69%	40.22%
Total	100.00%		100.00%	
Population	603,105	6.01%	688,601	9.29%

Others

	Male	% Change from 1980	Female	% Change from 1980
Age 0-18	36.24%	19.11%	35.33%	18.66%
Age 18-64	60.49%	36.55%	60.45%	37.67%
Age 65+	3.27%	25.79%	4.22%	32.60%
Total	100.00%		100.00%	
Population	123,833	29.33%	123,672	30.10%

tion category are the significant percentage increases in the age group under 18. This is the only population subgroup in Michigan that registers any positive increase in size since 1980 and is reflective of higher fertility levels and in-migration of families with young children.

To provide a more detailed perspective on population age compositional changes according to race and sex from 1980 to 1990, table 2 shows these changes for each of the Metropolitan Statistical Areas in Michigan. To give some idea of whether the percentage change is truly reflective of significant population change or whether it is tempered by relatively small underlying numbers, the absolute numerical change is given for each subcategory. From such a mass of numbers, the most easily identifiable trend is the com-

Table 2.

POPULATION CHANGE BY MSA, ETHNIC GROUP AND SEX: 1980-1990

Age Gp.	Black Females 0-14 Change	%	Black Females 15-65 Change	%	Black Females 65+ Change	%	Black Males 0-14 Change	%	Black Males 15-65 Change	%	Black Males 65+ Change	%
MSA												
Battle Creek	-50	-2.4498	223	4.9710	168	46.9274	60	2.9028	217	5.4007	77	35.1598
Benton Habor	-373	-8.2141	499	6.3069	182	33.7037	-532	-11.2545	173	2.8548	29	6.4159
Ann Arbor	-73	-1.8824	1587	15.9401	207	44.5161	-109	-2.744	1461	15.7844	134	43.5065
Detroit	-8857	-6.7667	30960	10.1752	11887	50.5658	-8672	-6.5341	13205	5.1008	5713	34.8694
Flint	-500	-3.8034	3305	12.4849	696	61.1062	-386	-2.9170	1195	5.2553	389	51.1842
Grand Rapids	1034	18.8103	3240	30.8337	279	47.1284	1268	23.2533	2988	33.1448	181	46.1735
Jackson	36	3.0560	307	13.7176	64	27.7056	87	7.9019	521	9.0735	83	64.8438
Kalamazoo	471	18.7202	1531	28.6222	123	46.7681	624	24.1486	1129	23.9601	32	17.3913
Lansing-East Lansing	778	21.2801	3162	38.9985	217	70.6840	943	25.8853	2605	36.3725	90	47.1204
Muskegon	85	2.6082	648	10.6544	224	51.9722	23	.7083	1257	23.8928	145	43.6747
Bay-Saginaw-Midland	-310	-4.8377	1119	9.0924	310	51.0708	-174	-2.6736	85	.8166	174	39.6355

Age Gp.	White Females 0-14 Change	%	White Females 15-65 Change	%	White Females 65+ Change	%	White Males 0-14 Change	%	White Males 15-65 Change	%	White Males 65+ Change	%
MSA												
Battle Creek	-1425	-10.5019	-2957	-7.0151	843	13.6143	-1458	-10.0358	-2867	-7.0820	600	16.1987
Benton Habor	-2605	-16.5114	-4540	-9.4312	1384	19.8252	-2739	-16.5169	-3922	-8.4493	1052	24.8876
Ann Arbor	-467	-2.2749	3926	4.6859	1501	22.4130	-337	-1.5446	2436	2.8479	895	24.3207
Detroit	-49876	-13.1470	-79159	-6.5872	31313	21.5524	-51647	-12.9115	-62154	-5.3093	15642	17.9696
Flint	-6788	-16.0092	-9246	-7.4294	2829	20.9602	-7741	-17.4465	-8463	-7.0880	970	12.0079
Grand Rapids	8251	12.9549	18089	9.6118	5745	23.6041	8260	12.3014	20467	11.3644	3619	25.5399
Jackson	-1611	-10.0839	-2034	-4.4708	1382	22.8657	-1615	-9.7348	-1014	-2.2011	975	27.8492
Kalamazoo	-538	-2.7947	1178	1.7168	2036	25.6520	-805	-3.9614	844	1.2798	1289	30.5523
Lansing-East Lansing	-2745	-6.6372	-190	-.1399	2933	22.2906	-3490	-8.0193	-1223	-.9329	1768	23.7762
Muskegon	-510	-3.3759	-2955	-6.4817	1693	27.0361	-454	-2.8402	-1172	-2.6992	1027	26.8076
Bay-Saginaw-Midland	-7766	-17.6753	-8433	-6.8048	4907	34.0409	-8374	-18.0716	-8170	-6.8047	2617	29.4608

plete *absence* of minus signs in the columns labeled "65+." Every MSA registered increases in the elderly population. For black males and females, the age group 16-64 has a similar lack of minus signs supporting the finding from table 1 that there was some growth in the black population between these ages. The remainder of the table is dominated by percentage declines. Young blacks and whites and working-age whites, male and female, are declining as a percentage of the population.

BIRTHS AND DEATHS IN MICHIGAN

A convenient way to assess the impact of fertility and mortality on population change is to examine the rate of natural increase. A population's natural increase is the excess of births over deaths, which is most conveniently expressed as a percentage rate. The rate of natural increase describes a population's "natural" growth unaffected by the impact of in-migration or out-migration. The salient characteristics of the rate of natural increase in Michigan's population between 1980 and 1990 are:
- The overall rate of natural increase of the state of Michigan was 6.69 percent; for non-metropolitan areas the rate was 5.49 percent, and for metropolitan areas it was 6.98 percent.
- At the individual county level, the rate of natural increase ranged from -8.35 percent in Keweenaw county in the Upper Peninsula, to 11.6 percent in Ottawa County in the southwest Lower Peninsula. In fact, the westernmost counties of the Upper Peninsula have either negative or very low positive rates of natural increase.
- Eight counties had negative rates of natural population increase: Keweenaw, Ontonagon, Gogebic and Iron (in the far west of the Upper Peninsula); Montmorency, Alcona and Roscommon (in the northeast Lower Peninsula); and Lake County.
- Forty-eight counties had rates of natural increase of between 5 percent and 10 percent, most of which are in the lower peninsula.

Figure 2 shows the rates of natural increase in population for each county in Michigan mapped according to five categories of percentage change. Apparent immediately is the fact that the vast majority of counties have positive rates of natural increase greater than 5 percent but less than 10 percent. Also, Ottawa and Kent counties stand

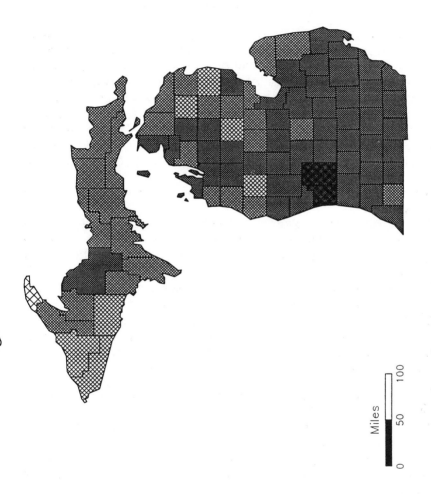

Figure 2.   Natural Increase Rates for Total Population in Michigan 1980-1990

out as the only counties with increases of over 10 percent. In overall terms, 30 counties experienced a population decline between 1980 and 1990, and 53 counties registered an increase in population.

NET MIGRATION IN MICHIGAN

The second component of overall population change is net migration, which is calculated by subtracting natural increase from population change and is also most often expressed as a percentage rate. Net migration is simply the difference between the number of people entering and leaving the state. Figure 3 continues the graphic mapping of the components of population change in Michigan by presenting net migration rates for each county. Overall, Michigan had a negative rate of net migration (-6.33 percent). The dominant patterns and trends in net migration at the county level in Michigan are:

- Between 1980 and 1990, 51 of Michigan's 83 counties experienced net out-migration.
- The counties that experienced significant in-migration (a net migration rate of greater than 10 percent) were those of the northern Lower Peninsula—the same counties that registered the greatest rate of natural increase.
- Bay, Saginaw, Genesee, Wayne, and Berrien counties in the Lower Peninsula had the greatest rates of out-migration.
- Luce county in the Upper Peninsula had the greatest rate of out-migration—over 15 percent. However, neighboring Chippewa County probably absorbed most of these migrants as it experienced an in-migration rate of over 15 percent.

It is likely that three trends will dominate net migration patterns in Michigan in the future:

- The industrialized counties in southern Michigan will continue to experience net out-migration.
- Those counties in northern Lower Peninsula with leisure/recreation as the major economic activity will continue to receive significant migration.
- The counties of the Upper Peninsula will continue to have a mixed pattern of migration with in-migration related to return migrants and retirees, and out-migration caused by the continuing decline of the industrial/employment base.

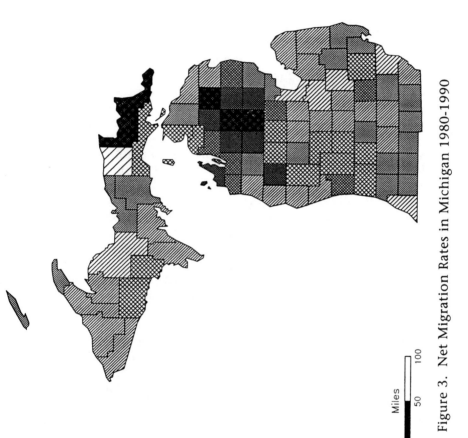

Figure 3.   Net Migration Rates in Michigan 1980-1990

It is difficult to present the disaggregation of county-level population change into its respective natural increase and net migration components in an intuitively understandable way because of the volume of data involved and the tremendous range in magnitude of change of each of the components. However, it is important to understand whether migration or natural increase contributed most to population increase or decrease at the sub-aggregate level. Tables 3a and 3b present a summary decomposition of overall population change for conventionally accepted regional divisions.[5]

Table 3a shows that of the 30 counties that experienced an overall population decline, 40 percent of them were located in the Upper Peninsula, over 23 percent were counties containing central cities of MSAs, and 20 percent were generally located in southern lower Michigan. The counties of northern lower Michigan were by far the largest share of the 53 counties that gained population between 1980 and 1990. What was the respective impact of natural increase and net migration on this population change? Despite the fact that 30 counties had an overall population decline, only 8 of Michigan's counties had a decline in natural increase; the vast majority of counties experienced natural population increase with almost 31 percent of those counties located in northern lower Michigan. The rightmost columns of table 3a show the dramatic impact of net migration of Michigan's regional population growth. Fifty-one counties had net *out-migration*, fairly evenly distributed over the five regions with the single exception that approximately only 12 percent of those 51 counties were metropolitan counties that do not contain central cities. In other words, out-migration is most dramatic from the most urbanized areas (counties with central cities of MSAs and counties in southern lower Michigan) and the most rural areas (the Upper Peninsula). Michigan is no less exempt from the "suburbanization" of population than any other region of America. Thirty-two counties experienced net in-migration with the lion's share of those counties, almost 60 percent, located in northern lower Michigan. Obviously, the regions with the highest out-migration had the lowest in-migration.

Table 3a can be rearranged to show the impact of the components of population change *within* each of the five major regional divisions. Some very interesting trends emerge from examining these figures. For example, of the 13 counties that make up the central counties region, the population change column shows that almost 54 percent of them had an overall population decline, none had an excess of deaths over births (i.e., negative natural increase), and a

Table 3a.

Population Change, Natural Increase/Decrease and Net Migration for major Regions of Michigan, 1980-1990

Region	Population change		Population Natural "Increase"		Migration		Total
	Decline	Increase	Decline	Increase	Decline	Increase	
Central Counties	23.33%	11.32%	0.00%	17.33%	23.53%	3.13%	13
Fringe Counties	3.33%	15.09%	0.00%	12.00%	11.76%	9.38%	9
Northern Lower Michigan	13.33%	43.30%	50.00%	30.67%	15.69%	59.38%	27
Southern Lower Michigan	20.00%	24.53%	0.00%	25.33%	27.45%	15.63%	19
Upper Peninsula	40.00%	5.66%	50.00%	14.67%	21.57%	12.50%	15
Total	100.00%	100.00%	100.00%	100.00%	100.00%	100.00%	100.00%
Michigan	30	53	8	75	51	32	83

Table 3b.

Population Change, Natural Increase/Decrease and Net Migration for Major Regions of Michigan,1980-1990

Region	Population change		Population Natural "Increase"		Migration		Total
	Decline	Increase	Decline	Increase	Decline	Increase	
Central Counties	53.85%	46.15%	0.00%	100.00%	92.31%	7.69%	13
Fringe Counties	11.11%	88.89%	0.00%	100.00%	66.67%	33.33%	9
Northern Lower Michigan	14.81%	85.19%	14.81%	85.19%	29.63%	70.37%	27
Southern Lower Michigan	31.58%	68.42%	0.00%	100.00%	73.68%	26.32%	19
Upper Peninsula	80.00%	20.00%	26.67%	73.33%	73.33%	26.67%	15
Michigan	30	53	8	75	51	32	83

Central counties contain central cities of MSAs: Bay, Berrien, Calhoun, Genesee, Ingham, Jackson, Kalamazoo, Kent, Midland, Muskegon, Saginaw, Washtenaw, and Wayne counties.
Fringe counties are metropolitan counties that do not contain central cities: Clinton, Eaton, Lapeer, Livingston,, Macomb, Monroe, Oakland, Ottawa, and St. Clair counties.
Northern Lower Michigan counties are: Alcona, Alpena, Antrim, Arenac, Benzie, Charlevoix, Cheboygan, Clare, Crawford, Emmet, Gladwin, Grand Traverse, Iosco, Kalkaska, Lake, Leelanau, Mason, Missaukee, Montmorency, Ogemaw, Osceola, Oscoda, Otsego, Presque Isle, Roscommon, and Wexford counties.
Southern Lower Michigan counties are: Allegan, Barry, Branch, Cass, Gratiot, Hillsdale, Huron, Ionia, Isabella, Lenawee, Mecosta, Montcalm, Newaygo, Oceana, St. Joseph, Sanilac, Shiawassee, Tuscola, and Van Buren counites.
The Upper Peninsula counties are: Alger, Baraga, Chippewa, Delta, Dickinson, Gogebic, Houghton, Iron, Keweenaw, Luce, Mackinac, Marquette, Menominee, Ontonagon, and Schoolcraft counties.

remarkable 92.31 percent (12 out of the 13 counties) had net out-migration. Obviously, the impact of net out-migration was more than compensating for the positive natural increase and was responsible for more than half of it, with an overall population decline. Although, the percentage of counties with an overall population decline was smaller among the "fringe " counties and among those of southern lower Michigan, the impact of out-migration also overwhelmed some of the natural increase population growth.

An interesting coincidence revealed in table 3b is that exactly the same percentage of counties in the Upper Peninsula experienced net out-migration and natural population increase. An examination of these counties reveals that the magnitude of the decrease through out-migration was substantially greater than the increase through an excess of births over deaths; in none of the counties in the Upper Peninsula was the outflow matched or exceeded by natural increase. The northern lower Michigan region contains 27 of Michigan's 83 counties and it is the only region where a majority of the counties registered a natural population increase (85.19 percent) *and* an increase through migration (70.37 percent). In terms of population change, the northern lower Michigan region is booming; a fact contributing significantly to the region's greater relative prosperity.

FERTILITY AND NUPTIALITY IN MICHIGAN

The aggregate, areal analysis of Michigan's demographic profile presented here could perhaps be elaborated upon by a refinement of the areal divisions or the calculation of additional aggregate population statistics; but such refinements would serve only to emphasize already observed trends and would add little to our existing knowledge. A superior approach is to focus on demographic indicators related to the vital processes underlying population change and to begin first with an examination of fertility and nuptiality in Michigan.

To give some indication of the change in trends over time, table 4 presents an array of indicators of fertility and nuptiality for Michigan at two points in time—1985 and 1990. There has been a mild uptick in the crude birth rate and a complementary increase in the other fertility indicators, the general fertility rate, and the total fertility rate. Despite this mild increase (which has been more substantial among black women), Michigan women's fertility is still significantly below a total fertility rate of 2.1, which would ensure

Table 4.

Changes in Selected Fertility & Nuptiality Indicators for Michigan 1985-1990.

Fertility Measures	1985	1990	% Change
Crude Birth Rate	15.2	16.5	8.55%
General Fertility Rate[1]			
White Females	62.07	64.60	4.08%
Black Females	71.11	93.10	30.92%
Total	63.60	69.10	8.65%
Total Fertility Rate[2]	1.77	1.82	3.05%
Abortion Rate			
(per 1000 women aged 15-44)	18.40	15.60	-15.22%
Number of Abortions			
(women aged 15-44)	41,400	34,655	-16.29%
Nuptiality Measures			
Number of Marriages	79,022	76,099	-3.69%
Marriage Rate	17.4	16.4	-5.74%
Number of Divorces	38,775	40,568	4.62%
Divorce Rate	8.5	8.7	2.35%

[1]The General Fertility Rate is expressed as the number of live birhs per 1000 women aged 15-44.
[2]The Total Fertility Rate is the number of births that women would have in their lifetime if, at each year of age, they experienced rates of childbearing occurring to women of that age in the specified year (U.S. Bureau of the Census, 1992). A TFR of 2.1 indicates a population is replacing itself.

replacement of the population. Both the number of abortions and the abortion rate among women aged 15 to 44 have decreased between 1985 and 1990. Two broad measures of nuptiality patterns show that in the last half of the decade the number of marriages (and the marriage rate) has seen a slight downturn, while the number of divorces (and the divorce rate) has seen an increase of a similar magnitude. These are indeed crude measures; they do not separate out first, second, or higher order marriages or divorces nor are controls for age, race, or any socioeconomic characteristic applied. However, in terms of the "big picture," Michigan does mirror the national trend toward a decline in marriage.

MORTALITY IN MICHIGAN

The examination of vital processes underlying population change is continued in table 5, which switches the focus to mortality indicators. The crude death rate decreased marginally between 1985 and

Table 5.
Changes in Selected Mortality Indicators for Michigan, 1985-1990.

Mortality Measures	1985	1990	% Change
Crude Death Rate	8.7	8.4	3.45%
Infant Mortality Rate			
Black	23.3	21.6	-7.30%
White	9.2	7.9	-14.13%
Other	6.0	6.9	15.00%
Total	11.4	10.4	-8.77%
Perinatal Mortality Rate	12.7	11.2	-11.81%
Neonatal Mortality Rate	7.8	7.2	-7.69%

Life Expectancy at Birth	1985			1990		
	Male	Female	Total	Male	Female	Total
White	71.2	78.0	74.6	73.1	78.8	75.9
All Others	63.9	73.1	68.5	62.3	71.4	66.9
Total	70.1	77.3	73.7	71.6	77.7	74.7

1990, while the infant mortality rate shows a more variable picture. The decline in the infant mortality rate among white infants is in excess of 14 percent while the rate among black babies declined by 7.3 percent and the rate for the "other" category increased by 15 percent, albeit from the overall lowest infant mortality rate of 6.0 per 1000 live births in 1985 to 6.9 in 1990. Two other infant mortality measures are presented to highlight the pattern of deaths very early in life. Deaths occurring during the first 12 months of life tend to be concentrated within the first week or month and the conventional infant mortality rate can be refined to reflect this increase in risk of death.

The neonatal mortality rate reflects deaths occurring with the first month of life and is usually expressed in terms of 1000 live births. In Michigan between 1985 and 1990 the neonatal mortality rate declined by 7.69 percent. One problem with infant mortality measures lies in defining what constitutes a live birth; errors often result from deliberate or inadvertent misclassification between fetal deaths, births, and neonatal deaths.[6] The perinatal mortality rate avoids the problem of defining a live birth and puts together late fetal and early neonatal deaths (i.e. still births and deaths to babies under one week old) and is expressed in terms of all births (still and live). In Michigan between 1985 and 1990, the perinatal mortality rate declined by almost 12 percent. These refined measures of early infant death were unavailable for different race or socioeconomic groups and just as there is variability in sub-groups' overall infant mortality rate decline, so too would we expect differences in these more refined measures.

The last measure of Michigan's mortality experience is the well-known indicator, life expectancy at birth, which states the average number of years a person born in a given year can expect to live. The bottom panel of table 5 presents life expectancy at birth for the total population, for males and females, and also for the white and non-white population. It is well known that the different risk of, and exposure to, different causes of death give women a superiority in life expectancy over men; a superiority which in Michigan ranges from 5.5 to 6 years for the total and white population, to 9.1 years in the non-white population in 1990. Perhaps the most striking finding in this panel is that the non-white population's life expectancy is so much lower than that of the white population, for both males and females, and the differential has widened from 1985 to 1990.

One final piece of information on mortality in Michigan, which is not presented in table 5, concerns the leading causes of death in the state. In 1990 the number one cause of death is heart disease, with a crude death rate of 296.1 per 100,000 of the population, followed by cancer (crude death rate, 198.1); and then a distant third and fourth are strokes (54.8), and accidents (33.7). Pulmonary chronic diseases, influenza/pneumonia, diabetes, cirrhosis, homicide, and suicide round out the top ten. This list of the top ten causes of death has remained fairly constant during the last decade.

SUMMARY

It has recently been noted that the policy uses of mortality data are likely to increase at the national and state levels because of greater statistical literacy among program planners, government and corporate executives, legislators, and the public at large.[7] This opinion is applicable to population data as a whole. Population data is now readily available, and with the application of basic geographic mapping technology trends and patterns it is readily discernible and can be used as input to informed policy decision making. Within Michigan, there have been several publications focusing on demographic data, its application to the provision of social services, its implications for current and future population trends, and its impact on state fiscal resources.[8]

In the 1980s, one of the earliest examples of policy-oriented work focused on the impact of immigration on receipt of general welfare in Michigan. Migration trends in the 1980s and changes in the allocation of general assistance have reduced this issue as a priority. But, concomitantly, preliminary analysis of the impact of the general assistance re-allocation policy in 1991 on former recipients of general assistance has indicated that the consequences of the withdrawal of general assistance were poorly anticipated and need now to be better understood.

Population projections for Michigan indicate that a modest but steady growth rate will continue into the next century. A total population of 10 million in 2010 is predicted, with the greatest *rates* of growth occurring, as expected, in northern lower Michigan, and the greatest *absolute number* increases (but smallest growth rates) occurring in the southern counties of the lower peninsula. It is projected that the distribution of population will not change radically from current patterns. One interesting projected statistic that summarizes much of the earlier discussion of the changing age composition is that the median age of Michigan's population will increase from 28.8 years in 1980, to 36 years in 2010; as of 1990, the median age of the state had already increased to 32.6 indicating that the pace of population aging is greater than originally anticipated.

This aging of the population will undoubtedly have implications for Michigan's Department of Social Services fiscal year appropriations. In 1992, medical services (expenditures on Medicaid and the State Medical Program) represented 52.5 percent of the total Department of Social Services budget.[9] The distribution of Medicaid funding will be influenced differentially by changes in the population age distribution and the associated changing health care utilization patterns. For example, institutional long-term care utilization is being replaced by community-based care utilization. Between 1980 and 1991 the use of community-based services has increased dramatically. Community-based Medicaid home health receipt has increased by 279 percent, and community-based home help has grown by 42 percent, between fiscal year 1980 and fiscal year 1991, while the use of institutional care has either declined or remained relatively stable.[10] These trends will continue in the future.

In short, Michigan's changing population mandates that increased importance be placed on the policy initiatives planned by state legislators and policymakers at all levels. The collection and disbursement of revenues; the demand for services, both social and economic; and the ability of Michigan to provide the requisite range of services is affected by the proportions of the population in the dependent and working ages, and these proportions will continue to swing away from the working ages to the upper extremes of the age distribution. The data is now available to monitor the causes and predicted paths of these distributional changes closely; the policy response is the challenge.

NOTES

1. B. Berelson, ed., *Population Policy in Developed Countries*, (New York: McGraw Hill, 1974).
2. The figures on labor force participation and poverty are taken from Michigan Population Update, Michigan Department of Management and Budget, Demographic Research and Statistics, June 1992.
3. For a comprehensive discussion of poverty based on the 1990 census, see "Portrait of America: A Time of Great Change and Growing Poverty," *The New York Times*, 29 May 1992.
4. For an multinational comparative assessment of the implications of increasing rates of disability, see "The Demography of Disability," Yeun-chung Yu, *Population Bulletin of the United Nations*, No. 30, 1991.
5. The regional divisions used for the decompositional analysis are those put forward by the Michigan Department of Management and Budget in *Population Projections for Michigan to the Year 2010*, summary report, March 1985.
6. See Henry S. Shryock and Jacob S. Siegel, *The Methods and Materials of Demography*, (condensed edition by Edward G. Stockwell), (New York: Academic Press, 1976), 245.
7. See Richard J. Havlik, "Death Data as Input to Policymaking," *Statistical Bulletin* (Jan-Mar, 1991): 27-35.
8. See Michigan Department of Social Services Information Packet, Policy Analysis Section Office of Planning, Budget and Evaluation, March 1992; Population Projections for Michigan to the Year 2000, summary report, Michigan Department of Management and Budget, 1985; Final Report on Immigration to Michigan by GA and ADC Recipients, Steve Smucker, Office of Planning, Budget and Evaluation, Michigan Department of Social Services; Michigan Population Update, Michigan Department of Management and Budget, Demographic Research and Statistics, June 1992.
9. See Michigan Department of Social Services Information Packet, Policy Analysis Section, Office of Planning, Budget and Evaluation. March 1992, 1.
10. Ibid., 55

Michigan Residents' Views on Policy Issues

Larry A. Hembroff, Timothy S. Bynum,
and Marcus Cheatham

INTRODUCTION

The very foundation of democratic society is the expression of the public's will. For the will of the people to result in a progressive improvement in the quality of life for the citizenry, it is essential for that citizenry to be well-informed—knowledgeable about situations at issue, the causes and consequences of events, and the possible impacts of alternative actions. In a *representative democracy* it is also essential that the "will of the people" be communicated to those elected to represent their views. But, herein lies the modern dilemma.

The numbers of people whom an elected representative is to represent far exceeds the number of individuals he or she can meet, let alone come to know. While we can presume that if an individual has been elected that at least a majority of his or her constituency believed he or she could best speak for them, political campaigns generally address policy issues in very broad strokes. Informing the electorate of candidates' views is far from complete (particularly for non-incumbents). Furthermore, many of the policy decisions on which representatives must make decisions could not be anticipated in the campaign or are too specific in their focus to receive attention in campaigns. The citizens may elect one candidate over another because they believe that, generally, that person's views are closer to their own. Still, on some specific issues, the majority may disagree with the representative.

So how do elected officials know the "will of the people" in order to represent their constituents? Many officials listen to the voices of people from their districts who call or visit their offices to express their concerns or wishes. Many officials attend or hold public meetings or visit schools or worksites within their districts. But those who write, those who call, those who attend public meetings, and those who schedule appointments to visit elected representatives are not a general cross-section of individuals in the district. Often those who speak to elected officials represent special interests—lobbyists paid to persuade officials to take the views of their group into account on a policy matter. Sometimes these views are at odds with the views of the majority, but the majority's views go unexpressed, in part, for lack of a direct communication link to the representative. This is the gap in the public policy process that survey research is well-suited to fill.

Properly executed, surveys can provide a relatively unbiased mechanism through which the public can inform government and elected officials of its wishes and needs. Through random sampling techniques, cross-sectional samples of the population can be selected which are very representative of the full population. Furthermore, since interviewers (typically) make repeated efforts to elicit the responses of individuals selected, there is generally more complete representation than is characteristic of many elections, particularly local and state elections where voter turn-out is conspicuously low. Some have even suggested that the application of survey methodologies represents the new form of democracy in America. To the extent this is becoming increasingly the case, the more important it is to consider the survey researcher's integrity, potential biases in application, the rigor of methods, and procedures used that affect the quality of the information.

This chapter reports the findings on several policy-related issues based on two surveys of Michigan adults conducted by MSU's Institute for Public Policy and Social Research (IPPSR). The issues include:
- Abortion
- Education
- Taxes and Government Spending
- Confidence in Public Institutions

ABOUT THE SURVEYS

The results we report are based on two random-digit dial telephone surveys of Michigan adults. The surveys were a part of IPPSR's Michigan Public Policy Survey series (MIPPS). Interviews for the initial MIPPS (MIPPS:1) were conducted between 12 April and 24 April 1992. In that time, IPPSR's Survey Research Division completed 993 interviews. The second survey, MIPPS:2, was conducted between 19 July and 4 August 1992. For this survey, interviewers completed 886 telephone interviews. In each survey, interviews lasting approximately 20 minutes in length were completed with a randomly selected resident 18 years of age or older in a random sample of Michigan households.

Households were selected for interviewing using random-digit dialing procedures. Approximately 96 percent of Michigan households have telephones; therefore, only a small amount of bias could occur due to inability to reach people because they lacked a telephone. The original sampling frame included all possible telephone numbers within the state. Blocks of phone numbers that contained no residential numbers or which contain only businesses or government offices were excluded. A random sample of numbers within blocks of working residential phone numbers was then selected for calling. Not all of these numbers were in service and some were assigned to businesses or other non-households. In the case that repeated calls to the selected number resulted in all no-answers—with a minimum of six call attempts—the number was discarded as being a non-working number.

In principle, 95 percent of all samples of this type and size should produce findings that differ from the findings reported here by no more than ±3.1 percentage points (for MIPPS:1) or ±3.3 percentage points (for MIPPS:2). That margin of variation, however, applies only to those questions answered by all respondents in the samples. For smaller segments of the samples, the potential margin of error is larger. Both samples closely approximate the demographic characteristics of the state's adult population, and have been weighted to adjust for sampling variation from the census profile of the state.

THE FINDINGS

ABORTION

Availability and funding of abortions remains a hotly argued policy issue in both Michigan and the Nation. For the past several years there have been efforts in the Michigan legislature to restrict access to abortions, especially for minors. There have been successful efforts to eliminate Medicaid funding of abortions. There have also been efforts to require minors to obtain parental consent or a waiver from a judge before they can have an abortion; to require a 24-hour waiting period; and to require that women seeking abortions receive information on abortions, including viewing pictures of fetuses. Some of these have been enacted, although a Kalamazoo judge stayed the implementation until recently.

To examine the citizenry's views on these issues several questions regarding these were posed in the MIPPS:2 interview. The first question was posed as follows:

> Recently, the Supreme Court reaffirmed the right of a woman to terminate her pregnancy. The court also upheld a Pennsylvania law that put regulations on abortions, such as a 24-hour waiting period, spousal notification, and providing abortion information including photos of fetuses. In general, do you agree with the Supreme Court that states have the right to place regulations on abortions?

Overall, 43.7 percent of the respondents indicated that they agreed, but the majority, 54.1 percent, indicated that they disagreed. Presumably, those disagreeing were indicating a view that states should not be able to put restrictions on the availability or access to abortions. Michigan adults living outside the Detroit Metropolitan area (i.e., Wayne, Oakland, and Maccomb counties) were more likely to agree with the Supreme Court ruling (47.2 percent of residents in rural counties; 51.2 percent in other urban counties) than were those living in the Metro area (32.9 percent of residents in the City of Detroit; 35.1 percent of residents.of Maccomb, Oakland, and Wayne, counties excluding Detroit). Similarly, males were more likely to agree with the Supreme Court ruling than were females (48.3 percent vs. 39.8 percent). And white respondents were more likely to agree with the ruling (46.5 percent) than were either African American (28.1 percent) or respondents of other racial groups (39.7 percent). There were no significant differences in their views among respondents based on their household incomes.

MIPPS:2 included a general question regarding the respondents' views on the availability of abortions. Respondents were asked to indicate which of the following came closest to representing their views on abortion:

Abortion should generally be available.

Abortion should be available but under stricter limits
   than it is now

Abortion should not be permitted.

Responses were generally consistent with those to the first question. Overall, 43.9 percent of respondents indicated that "abortions should generally be available" (see Figure 1). Only 17.2 percent said that "abortions should not be permitted" and a little more than a third of the respondents (37.8 percent) said that "abortion should be permitted but under stricter limits than it is now."

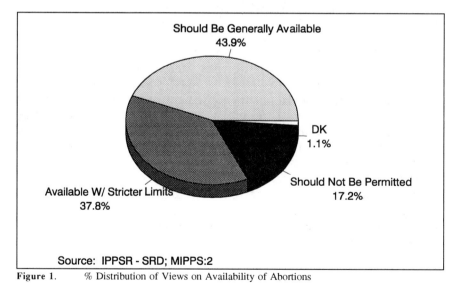

Should Be Generally Available
43.9%

DK
1.1%

Should Not Be Permitted
17.2%

Available W/ Stricter Limits
37.8%

Source: IPPSR - SRD; MIPPS:2

Figure 1.   % Distribution of Views on Availability of Abortions

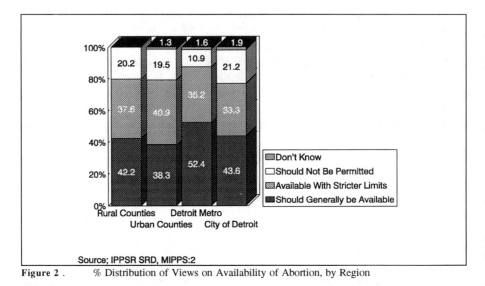

Figure 2 .   % Distribution of Views on Availability of Abortion, by Region

Figure 2 shows the percentages of respondents claiming each of the views within the rural counties of Michigan, the urban counties outside of the Detroit Metro area, the Metro area counties excluding the City of Detroit, and within Detroit itself. The figure indicates that respondents in the Metro area excluding Detroit were less likely than other Michigan residents to believe that abortions should not be allowed. They were also more likely than other Michigan residents to believe that abortions should be generally available. There were no differences between males and females or among racial groups in terms of the distributions of their views on this question. There were differences, however, across income categories with higher income respondents being somewhat more likely than others to favor having abortions generally available and less likely than others to believe that abortions should not be allowed.

For those who had indicated that they thought abortions should be available but under stricter limits than exist currently, we asked several follow-up questions about possible restrictions. These respondents were asked if they supported a requirement of parental notification, a 24-hour waiting period, or providing abortion information that included viewing pictures of fetuses. Figure 3 shows the percentages of those favoring stricter limits who indicated support for each of these specific regulations. The figure shows that 87.5 percent of these respondents supported the requirement of parental notifica-

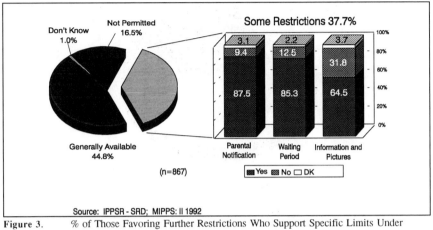

Figure 3.   % of Those Favoring Further Restrictions Who Support Specific Limits Under Consideration

tion, 85.3 percent supported the requirement of a 24-hour waiting period, and 64.5 percent supported the mandatory presentation of information on abortions. It is important to recall that these still represent a minority of all respondents. That is, considering the numbers of respondents who said that abortions should be available generally without further restrictions and those that said it should not be available at all, the percentage of all respondents favoring each of these additional restrictions was 33.6 percent, 33.0 percent, and 24.8 percent respectively.

There were no significant differences between males and females in the percentages supporting each of these requirements. There were significant differences among racial groups, with African Americans consistently less likely to support adding the restriction than were white or other racial group respondents.

The final question on abortion asked respondents who should be responsible, primarily, for making rules regarding access to abortion. Interviewers gave respondents a choice among the Supreme Court, the U.S. Congress, the state legislatures, or no one. Figure 4 shows the percentages of all respondents choosing each of the options. The figure clearly indicates that the most common response (48.8 percent) was that "no one" should make rules regarding access to abortion. More respondents thought state legislatures (15.8 percent) should be responsible for making such rules than thought it belonged to the

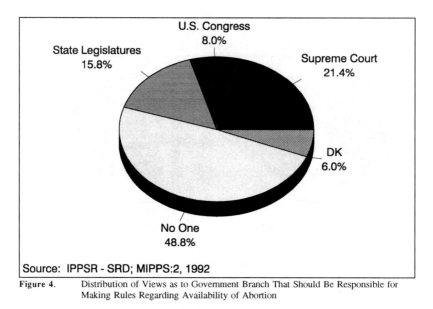

Figure 4.   Distribution of Views as to Government Branch That Should Be Responsible for Making Rules Regarding Availability of Abortion

Congress (8.0 percent), but both of these were lower percentages than thought the Supreme Court should be primarily responsible (21.4 percent) and far lower than the percentage that thought no one should be responsible for making such rules. Females (52.3 percent) were more likely than males (44.7 percent) to say they thought *no one* should be responsible for making rules about access to abortion, as were African American respondents (55.4 percent) compared to white (47.8 percent) and other racial group respondents (44.3 percent).

In summary, Michigan adults generally support having abortions available to women. Furthermore, there appeared to be little support among the whole population for adding restrictions that might limit that access. Among the three requirements that have been actively under consideration by the Michigan legislature, least supported was the one requiring that women seeking abortions look at information about abortions, including viewing photographs of fetuses. Relatively few respondents thought legislatures should be responsible for making rules about access to abortion.

EDUCATION

For more than a decade, the quality of public education has been the focus of considerable discussion. Scores on standardized tests

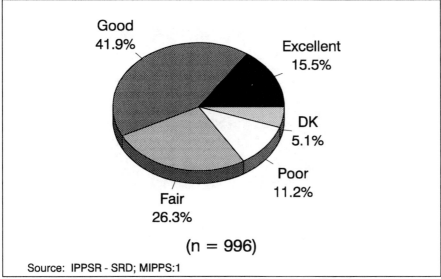

Good
41.9%

Excellent
15.5%

DK
5.1%

Poor
11.2%

Fair
26.3%

(n = 996)

Source: IPPSR - SRD; MIPPS:1

Figure 5.   % Distribution of Opinions on the Quality of Local Public Schools

such as the SAT have continued to erode, at least on verbal ability. In Michigan, two issues have been of particular concern: the *quality* of public education, and the *funding* of public education. The two issues are bound together in highly complex ways. Recently, one of Michigan's school districts chose to close its schools for the year ten weeks early because it could not afford to keep the schools open any longer without severely cutting back on the programs the district regarded as essential to a quality education. Questions about these two issues were included in MIPPS:1.

All 996 respondents were asked *"In general, would you say the public schools where you live are excellent, good, fair, or poor?"* Figure 5 shows the distribution of responses. The figure indicates that only about one in seven respondents (15.5 percent) rated their local public schools as "excellent," while more than a third judged their local schools as fair (26.3 percent) or poor (11.2 percent). However, there were statistically significant differences among segments of the population as to how they rated their local schools.

Figures 6 and 7 show the distributions of ratings for the four geographic areas and for different income groups of respondents. Figure 6 indicates that the ratings were very similar across all regions of the state except for in the City of Detroit where nearly three quarters of all respondents judged the local schools as either "fair" (41.6 percent) or "poor" (32.0 percent).

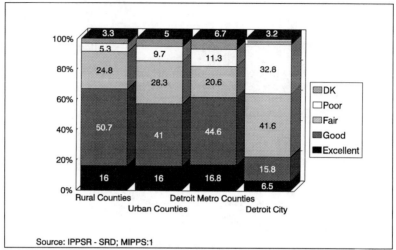

Source: IPPSR - SRD; MIPPS:1

Figure 6 .   Rating of Local Public Schools, by Region

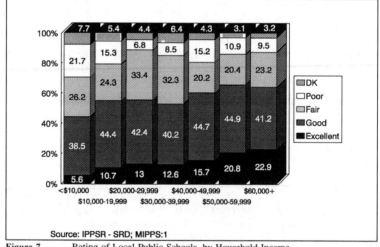

Source: IPPSR - SRD; MIPPS:1

Figure 7.   Rating of Local Public Schools, by Household Income

Figure 7 indicates that the percentages of respondents who judged their local schools as "excellent" increased as household income increased. While there is considerable heterogeneity within most communities with respect to income levels, it is also the case that some communities are much more affluent than others. Given that property taxes are the principle funding sources for public schools in the state, then some communities can afford to fund their schools at much higher levels than others and can provide qualitatively different educational experiences for their children. The differences in these ratings across income groups shown in Figure 7 no doubt *partially* reflects the resulting actual differences in educational quality.

It is this inequality of educational opportunity that is partly the basis of the debate about the funding of education in Michigan. To examine public sentiment on this issue, interviewers asked respondents the following question:

> Do you feel that the current method of funding public schools in Michigan through property taxes is a good way or do you think that public school funding should be equalized through a method of statewide funding?

Among all respondents, less than a quarter (21.6 percent) indicated that they thought the current method of funding was a good way, while *two out of three respondents (66.4 percent) indicated that they thought funding should be equalized through a method of statewide funding* (see Figure 8). Not surprisingly, respondents who were more likely to be living in communities that can afford to fund education at higher levels tended to be less dissatisfied with the current funding method than other respondents.

Figures 9 and 10 show the differences in responses among respondents of different racial groups and different regions of the state. Figure 9 indicates that African American and Other racial group respondents were significantly more likely to say that funding should be equalized, while white respondents were more likely than

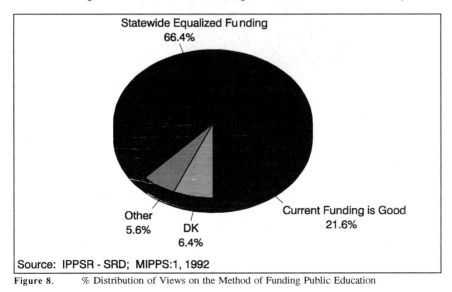

Source: IPPSR - SRD; MIPPS:1, 1992

Figure 8.   % Distribution of Views on the Method of Funding Public Education

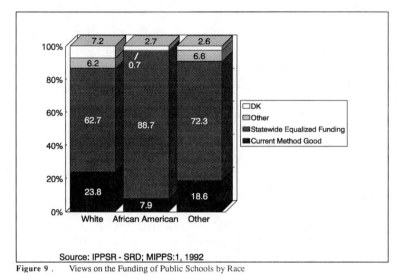

Source: IPPSR - SRD; MIPPS:1, 1992

Figure 9 .   Views on the Funding of Public Schools by Race

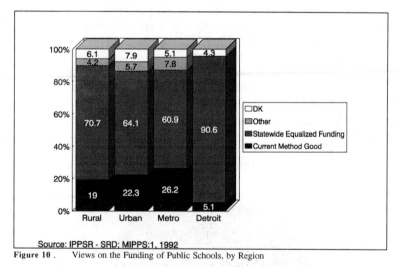

Source: IPPSR - SRD; MIPPS:1, 1992

Figure 10 .   Views on the Funding of Public Schools, by Region

their counterparts to say that the current method of funding is a good method.

Similarly, Figure 10 shows that the percentages of respondents who said that funding should be equalized was greatest among residents of Detroit followed by those of rural counties. The percentage who thought funding should be equalized was lowest among respondents living in the Detroit Metro area excluding the city of Detroit. One of these, Oakland County, is the most affluent county in the entire state. To some extent, these are the counties where the residents' property tax monies might be expected to be redistributed to other parts of the state under a policy change that would equalize funding across school districts in the state.

In summary, the results of MIPPS:1 indicated that nearly as many Michigan residents believe the public schools are "poor" as "excellent." The survey also found that dissatisfaction with the public schools was greater in Detroit than elsewhere and was greater among lower income respondents. The survey also found widespread preference for reform of the school finance mechanism in the state with a funding policy that equalizes funding across the state preferred.

TAXES AND GOVERNMENT SPENDING

The concern about the financing of public education is a specific example of a more general concern about taxes and spending in the state. For each of the past several years, the state of Michigan has wrestled with projected revenue shortfalls and has had to cut back significantly on state programs including general assistance welfare in order to balance the state budget. The weak domestic auto performance and the auto industry's major role in the state's economy has contributed substantially to the budget situation.

Faced with continuing revenue shortfalls, the state has two basic choices: to cut spending by reducing services and programs, or to raise additional revenues with tax increases. In MIPPS:1, we queried respondents as to their preference given this choice. The question was posed as follows:

> Like many states, Michigan faces the problem of not having enough tax money to pay for the various services and programs that the state government provides. One way to solve this problem is to raise taxes. Another way to resolve the problem is to reduce state services and programs. Which do you prefer—raising taxes or reducing services and programs?

Figure 11 shows the results among respondents throughout the state. The figure indicates that respondents favored reducing services and programs over raising taxes by a five-to-three margin (46.7 percent vs. 29.2 percent). The figure also indicates that 3.7 percent of respondents said they would prefer doing both—raising taxes and

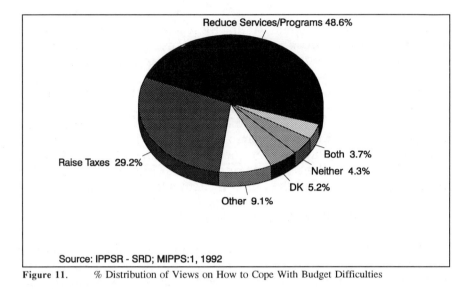

Source: IPPSR - SRD; MIPPS:1, 1992

Figure 11.   % Distribution of Views on How to Cope With Budget Difficulties

cutting spending; while 4.3 percent indicated they would prefer neither; and more than one in ten indicated preferring still other
options (11.0 percent) such as reducing waste.

Views on resolving the budget dilemma differed among some segments of the state's population. African American respondents and
residents of Detroit were much more likely than others to prefer raising taxes and less likely to prefer reducing state services and programs. These are illustrated in Figures 12 and 13. Figure 12 indicates
that 54.2 percent of African American respondents said they would
prefer to raise taxes, compared to only 25.8 percent of white respondents and 25.4 percent of respondents of other racial groups.
Conversely, 49.0 percent of white respondents and 58.4 percent of
other racial group respondents indicated they would prefer to have
services and programs cut compared to only 20.4 percent of African
Americans.

Similarly, Figure 13 indicates that 60.6 percent of respondents
from Detroit would prefer to have taxes raised compared to only
23.1 percent of respondents from rural counties, 28.6 percent of
respondents from non-Metro urban counties, and 25.6 percent of
respondents from the three Detroit metro counties excluding the
city. The figure shows that nearly half of the respondents from these
latter three regions preferred reducing spending for services and programs, while only 13.1 percent of respondents from Detroit preferred this option.

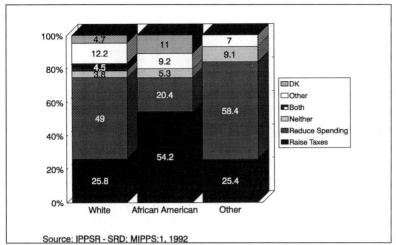

Source: IPPSR - SRD; MIPPS:1, 1992

Figure 12 .   Distribution of Views on Handling Budget Difficulties, by Race

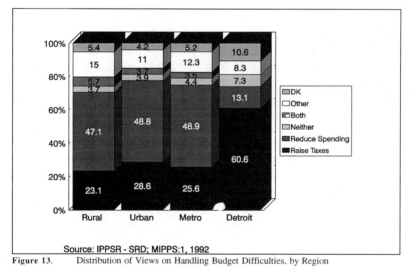

Source: IPPSR - SRD; MIPPS:1, 1992

Figure 13.   Distribution of Views on Handling Budget Difficulties, by Region

Respondents were asked what their preferences would be if raising taxes could not be avoided. Respondents were presented with the following question:

> If taxes do have to be raised, there are several different methods that might be used. Please tell me if you would favor or oppose using the following methods if tax money does have to be raised.

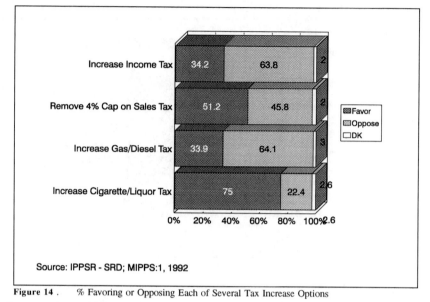

Source: IPPSR - SRD; MIPPS:1, 1992

Figure 14 .   % Favoring or Opposing Each of Several Tax Increase Options

Respondents were presented with "an increase in the state income tax," "removing the 4 percent cap on state sales tax," "an increase in gasoline and diesel fuel tax," and "an increase in cigarette and liquor taxes." Figure 14 shows the results. As the figure clearly shows, the tax increase that was most palatable to respondents was an increase in the tax on cigarettes and alcohol—sometimes referred to as "sin taxes." Only approximately one quarter of the adults in Michigan smoke and, although roughly nine out of ten adults consume alcohol, most consume relatively modest amounts rather infrequently. Therefore, increasing the taxes on these would either not affect most adults or they could control the amount of tax they pay by limiting how much alcohol they drink. Thus, it is not surprising that three quarters of respondents indicated they would favor increasing these taxes if taxes had to be raised. It would be much less easy for individuals to avoid an increase in the amount of taxes they pay annually with each of the other possible options.

Of the other tax increases listed, the least palatable was an increase in the taxes on gasoline and diesel fuel (33.9 percent favor; 64.1 percent oppose), followed closely by an increase in the state income tax (34.2 percent favor; 63.8 percent oppose). Figure 14 indicates that a simple majority (51.2 percent) indicated favoring a removal of the 4 percent cap on the state sales tax.

In summary, peoples' views on raising taxes versus cutting government services and programs tended to reflect their self-interests, but only partially. Those population segments or geographic areas that would likely experience the greatest loss by cutbacks in government spending also tended to favor raising taxes, while the tax increase most favored was that which would not affect most of the population or was controllable by the individuals affected. On the other hand, the second most favored tax—an increase in the sales tax—is generally regarded as being regressive, representing a larger portion of the resources of those with lower incomes. Another regressive tax, increasing gasoline and diesel fuel taxes, was the least favored option, while the most progressive tax option listed—increasing the income tax—was opposed by two-thirds of respondents.

CONFIDENCE IN INSTITUTIONS

We began this essay discussing the role of surveys in democratic societies. We also suggested that the communication of citizens' views and wishes was critical for policymakers to be representative. Implicitly, at least, we suggested that the more difficult it is for elected officials to hear about the views and wishes of representative cross-sections of their constituencies, the more likely they may be to vote on bills in ways that are at odds with the majority in their districts. We also implied that this may be more likely as the size and complexity of the population officials represent increases or as they become physically and socially more distant from the electorate. One way to examine the extent to which this may be true would be to ask individuals how confident they are in various kinds of public institutions. If what we have suggested is correct, we should expect a greater degree of confidence in those institutions with which individuals may have more direct contact or control.

In MIPPS:2, we asked respondents to indicate how much confidence they had in a variety of organizations and institutions. For each one, respondents were asked whether they had a great deal of confidence, quite a lot, some, very little, or none. Figure 15 shows the results. We have elected to not show the percentages that indicated "very little" or "none" as their response to make the comparison among institutions more readily interpretable.

Figure 15 indicates that, generally, more respondents had confidence in those organizations and institutions that were more nearly locally based than those at the national level. Respondents indicated having the greatest confidence in religious organizations, such as the Salvation Army, that operate locally. Confidence declined among

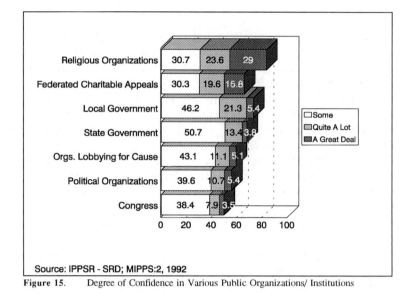

Source: IPPSR - SRD; MIPPS:2, 1992

Figure 15.   Degree of Confidence in Various Public Organizations/ Institutions

those organization's or institution's with broader foci. For example, local governments received greater confidence than did state government, and state government received greater confidence than did the Federal government.

Confidence was also higher for organizations ostensibly trying to help others—such as federated charitable appeals like United Way— than for organizations trying to help themselves or their own members, such as lobbyist organizations. In light of this, it is particularly interesting that political organizations, like Republicans and Democrats, and the Congress, received the lowest degree of confidence of those presented to respondents. This suggests that citizens believe that the actions of these are driven by parochial interests that may be at odds with the interests or views of the general citizenry, or that citizens have less input or control over their actions.

While the relatively higher overall confidence rating of state government, compared to federal government and nationally-focused institutions is probably good news for state government, there also appears to be some room for improvement. Furthermore, the interview questions did not try to differentiate confidence in the legislature, versus the governor's office, versus the state bureaucracy, or among the various state departments. Clearly, one gathers from talking to neighbors and associates that there are differing degrees to which these various branches and departments are perceived to be responsive to citizens' interests and wishes. For purposes of reform or continuing development, further research that would establish the level of citizen confidence in these bodies, the reasons for their lack of confidence when it is low, and overall assessments of their performances would be valuable. Identifying mechanisms through which the structures and operations of government can be more responsive to the needs and wishes of the citizenry would be a tremendous service to the state.

CONCLUSION

This chapter has summarized the results of two public policy surveys conducted by the Survey Research Division of MSU's Institute for Public Policy and Social Research. The surveys focused on Michigan citizens' views on policy questions related to abortion, the funding of public education, and taxes. In the analysis, we have examined regional, racial, gender, and income differences in views on these issues.

The analyses indicated that support for the various policy initiatives or options varied to some extent across segments of the population. In some instances, as in the case of increasing the restrictions on access to abortions, the actions of the legislature appear to be at odds with the views of at least a plurality of Michigan adults.

The analysis found much greater dissatisfaction with the quality of public education among individuals in Detroit than elsewhere in the state, but the survey found widespread dissatisfaction with the current mechanisms for funding education. Although stronger among some groups than others, there was a preference for an alternative statewide funding system that would make funding more equitable across school districts. This preference was shared by all regions of the state, all racial groups, and all income groups.

The analysis also examined preferences regarding how the state should deal with budget shortfalls. Whereas the majority of African Americans and residents of Detroit would prefer to resolve a deficit by raising taxes, the majority of other residents and those in other regions of the state would prefer to cut back programs and reduce spending. If tax increases are necessary, a large majority of residents would prefer increased taxes on alcohol and tobacco while a slim majority would favor an increase in the sales tax. Substantial majorities opposed increases in the income tax or the taxes on gasoline and diesel fuels as ways to increase revenues.

The analysis also found that there was considerable variation in the level of confidence residents had in public institutions or organizations. For the most part, residents claimed to have more confidence in institutions with which they have greater opportunities for direct communication and those that are less likely to be promoting special interests, e.g., local governments, churches, charitable organizations. On the other hand, institutions or organizations with national foci, or which are perceived to promote special interests, enjoyed much less confidence on the part of Michigan residents. We suggested that the lower level of confidence may reflect a weakness in the communication links through which residents can express their views to representatives on policy matters.

In any year, policies are formulated, modified, or abandoned at all levels of government and among all branches of government. The extent to which these policy actions express the preferences of the citizenry is not only likely to affect the confidence of the citizenry in public institutions, it is also the measure of the degree to which the policymaking process is democratic.

We have suggested that survey research can assist in communicating the citizenry's preferences to their elected officials, but this is not without limits. The utility of surveys for this purpose depends on how well informed the public is of the issues. But, as technology and issues become increasingly complex—as the systemic nature of many social problems becomes recognized—one wonders, what are the limits of the public's ability or motivation to understand the causes of problems and the implications of policy options?

Is there a difference between seeking public input in the policy decision process and simply trying to do the popular thing? Will it be the right thing? If survey research can play such a communicative role, how often can the citizenry be surveyed? What are the limits of survey research in framing the most appropriate questions that get to the heart of a policy issue? Are there policy questions that, by their nature, cannot be reduced to the kind of questions that can be asked in a general population survey? The answers to these questions depend in large measure on the creativity, integrity, and methodological practices of those conducting the surveys. It also depends on the public's understanding of surveys as a vehicle through which to express their needs and preferences to public officials and their ability to differentiate such surveys from a sales pitch or a plea for money.

Racial Differences in Mortality in Michigan: Are African Americans Better Off Now Than in 1960?

Bruce A. Christenson and Nan E. Johnson

I. THE PROBLEM

Mortality is a fundamental indicator of the quality of life and health of a population. Thus, the relatively high levels of mortality among African Americans is a matter of national concern.[1] The available evidence indicates that it should also be a matter of concern for the State of Michigan. Upon entering the final decade of the twentieth century, Michigan's African American population is experiencing a substantially higher level of mortality than the white population. Adjusting for the younger average age of African Americans, initial 1989-90 estimates for Michigan indicate that the overall death rate is 46 percent higher for black males as compared to white males, and 27 percent higher for black females as compared to white females.[2] Moreover, the following analysis suggests that there is a growing difference between African Americans and whites in the average length of life in Michigan. Whereas in the early 1960s, it appeared that Michigan's racial gap in expected length of life was substantially smaller than racial differences at the national level, this is no longer the case.

II. KEY POLICY QUESTIONS

Some of the important policy issues raised by the relatively high levels of mortality among African Americans in Michigan include the following:

- What impact does mortality have on the average length of life of the African American population, and how does this compare to the white population?
- How has the impact of mortality changed for African Americans since 1960?
- What are the principal causes of death that most adversely affect the lives of African Americans, and do these causes similarly affect whites?

III. STATE OF AFFAIRS

LIFE EXPECTANCY AT BIRTH

The higher rates of mortality among African Americans in Michigan create a tangibly shorter expected length of life in comparison to the white population. At current mortality rates, the life expectancy from birth of African American males in Michigan is 65.2 years as compared to 73.2 years for white males. African American females in Michigan have a life expectancy of 74 years as compared to 79.5 years for white females. In other words, the average length of life expected for African Americans in Michigan is eight years shorter than that of whites in the case of males and 5.5 years shorter in the case of females (Table 1).[3]

A review of decennial estimates of life expectancies for African American males in Michigan over the last 30 years presents a disturbing picture, whether viewed separately or in comparison to white males (Table 1). In the early 1960s, the life expectancy of Michigan's non-white male population, of whom nearly 97 percent were black, was 65.2 years from birth. The national life expectancy for African American males at that time was shorter by over three years.[4] One decade later, the life expectancy of Michigan's black male population had slipped to less than 63 years of life. It rebounded to 65.5 years at the beginning of the 1980s. By that time, however, the difference between Michigan and the rest of the country in life expectancy of African American males had diminished to only a half-year lead for

Table 1.
Life Expectancy at Birth by Gender, Race, and Period
of Observation for Michigan Residents

Subgroup	1959-61	1969-71	1979-81	1989-90
Males				
Blacks	65.20	62.81	65.49	65.18
Whites	67.87	68.35	71.08	73.20
Difference	-2.67	-5.54	-5.59	-8.02
Females				
Blacks	69.32	71.59	73.70	73.99
Whites	74.39	75.77	78.30	79.46
Difference	-5.07	-4.18	-4.60	-5.47

Note: Mortality data by age, race, and sex for 1959-61, 1969-71, and 1979-81 are from *Vital Statistics of the United States, Volume II, Mortality, Part B.* Since mortality data on Michigan residents for 1989-90 were yet unpublished, these data were obtained by the authors from a data tape released for their use by the Michigan Department of Public Health. Because mortality data were not published separately for blacks in the 1959-61 and 1969-71 periods, we used mortality data on non-whites as proxies for those of blacks.

---

the state. The estimates of current life expectancy for Michigan indicate no further improvement.

In brief, the life expectancy at birth for Michigan's black males has not shown any sustained progress for three decades. Placed in historical perspective, the current life expectancy for the African American male population of Michigan is no better than it was before the Great Society legislation and the civil rights reforms enacted in the 1960s.

During this same period, the life expectancy at birth for white males increased steadily from slightly less than 68 years to over 73 years at present (Table 1). Racial differences in mortality at the beginning of the 1960s resulted in a 2.7-year difference in life expectancy between black and white males. By comparison, the national racial difference in life expectancy was almost six years. However, Michigan's racial gap for males expanded to match the national level over the next two decades. At the beginning of the 1980s, the racial difference in male life expectancy from birth was 5.6 years in Michigan as compared to the national difference of 5.8 years.[5] The current 8-year racial difference in life expectancy among males in Michigan is about triple the difference that existed three decades ago.

This may also be larger than the racial difference at the national level, which in 1988 was reported as a difference of 7.4 years.[6]

The absolute changes in life expectancy at birth for African American females are more favorable than for African American males, although conditions relative to white females have not improved. In the early 1960s, the life expectancy of non-white females, of whom over 97 percent were black, was about 69 years. This was almost three years longer than the national life expectancy for black females.[7]

The decennial figures suggest that during the next two decades the life expectancy of black females in Michigan increased steadily, reaching 73.7 years by 1980. The life expectancy of African American females increased even more rapidly at the national level. By 1980 only about a one-half year difference was found in Michigan and the national-level life expectancy of African American females. The estimated current life expectancy of 74 years for Michigan's black female population indicates that there was considerably slower improvement in overall mortality conditions in the 1980s as compared to the preceding decade.

The life expectancy of Michigan's white female population was 74.4 years in the early 1960s, leaving that group with a 5-year advantage relative to black females in Michigan. By comparison, the national-level racial difference at that time showed white females with an 8-year advantage relative to black females.[8] Modest declines in this racial difference at the state level over the next two decades reflected a slightly faster level of improvement in life expectancy of black females relative to white females. Declining female racial differences at the national level were even more rapid. By the beginning of the 1980s, the racial gap in life expectancy was 4.6 years in Michigan as compared to a national-level racial gap of five years.

As a result of faster improvements in life expectancy for Michigan's white females during the 1980s, the racial gap in female life expectancy in Michigan has widened again to 5.5 years. This is actually somewhat wider than the racial gap that existed in the early 1960s. Nationally, published reports from 1988 estimate recent female racial differences in life expectancy to be about 5.5 years.[9] Thus, Michigan's racial gap in female life expectancy at the end of the 1980s equaled the national gap.

In summary, the gap in life expectancy of blacks in Michigan relative to whites has increased over the past 30 years; this increase has been particularly large in the case of males. A more detailed understanding of these trends may be obtained by focusing on selected age groups and by considering the impact of some of the principal causes of death. The following sections examine these issues.

PREMATURE MORTALITY

While death is recognized as an inevitable event, its occurrence in contemporary society is generally expected to be postponed until late in life. Many causes of death that strike throughout the life cycle have long been recognized as preventable (e.g., accidents, homicides, and suicides) or treatable to varying extents (e.g, chronic diseases). Recognition of the increasing ability of many individuals to postpone death until very old ages and to remain economically productive until quite late in life has led public health researchers to define death before age 70 as premature mortality.[10]

Infant Mortality Rates

Infancy, the period between birth and completion of the first year of life, is the most perilous stage of childhood. If the prevention of premature deaths is an important public health objective, reducing rates of infant mortality is clearly an important focus for public officials. Its significance has been highlighted in recent years by more public awareness of wide racial disparities in national infant mortality rates.[11]

African Americans in Michigan are currently experiencing 20 infant deaths for every 1,000 live births in the case of female infants, and 23 deaths for every 1,000 live births in the case of male infants (Table 2). Among whites, the rates are 7 deaths per 1,000 births for females and 9 deaths per 1,000 births for males. Between 13 and 14 more African American infants are dying per 1,000 births as compared to white infants of the same sex.

Male and female infant mortality rates declined steadily between 1960 and 1980 for both races. From 1959-61, an estimated 41 black male infants died for every 1,000 born alive.[12] In contrast, the infant mortality rate was 26 per 1,000 live births for white males. By 1979-81, the infant mortality rate of black males had been reduced to 26 per 1,000 live births, whereas that of white males had fallen to slightly over 12 per 1,000 births. The racial disparity in infant mortality rates declined slightly during this period from 15 to about 13 more deaths per 1,000 among black male infants as compared to white male infants. A similar pattern of change exists with respect to racial differences in mortality of female infants.

Table 2.

Infant Mortality Rates by Gender, Race, and Period of Observation
for Michigan Residents

Subgroup	1959-61	1969-71	1979-81	1989-90
Males
Blacks	40.7	33.8	25.8	23.0
Whites	25.6	20.4	2.4	9.0
Difference	15.1	13.4	13.4	14.0
Females
Blacks	33.0	28.1	22.1	20.3
Whites	19.3	15.5	9.6	7.1
Difference	13.7	12.6	12.5	13.2

Note: Infant mortality rates (IMRs) are expressed as the number of deaths to persons under age one year per 1,000 live births in the same historical period. Death counts can fluctuate annually due to epidemics. Birth counts can vary annually due to changes in the spacing of births. Thus, to add stability to the calculated rate, each IMR before 1989 was based on three consecutive years of infant death data and birth data: $((D_1 + D_2 + D_3)/(B_1 + B_2 + B_3)) \times 1000$. Data on infant deaths by race and sex for 1959-61, 1969-71, and 1979-81 are from the annual series *Vital Statistics of the United States, Volume II, Mortality, Part B*. Because mortality data were not published separately for blacks in the 1959-61 and 1969-71 periods, we used mortality data on non-whites as proxies for those of blacks. Data on births for these time periods are from the annual series *Vital Statistics of the United States, Volume 1, Natality*. At this writing, the vital statistics for 1989 and 1990 were yet unpublished. The death counts were obtained from a data tape released by the Michigan Department of Public Health (MDPH) for use by the authors. The birth counts by race and sex for 1989, and by sex for 1990 were supplied to the authors by Kathy Humphrys of MDPH in a telephone conversation on 24 July 1992. For the purpose of computing the 1989-90 race-sex specific IMRs, we assumed that the racial composition of male births and female births in 1990 was the same as in 1989. In 1989, children of mixed-raced parentage were classified according to the mother's race; but to maintain consistency with the previous classification system, we tabulated them according to the race of the minority parent.

Further decline in infant mortality rates from 1979-81 to 1989-90 was small in contrast to preceding decennial changes, particularly for blacks (Table 2). The slowed improvement may reflect the impact of a severe economic recession in the state economy in the early 1980s. The loss of jobs and rising cost of health care likely exacerbated the problems of maintaining the health insurance needed to insure access to adequate and timely pre- and postnatal health care.

Reduction of federal support for state food programs may also have jeopardized efforts to improve the adequacy of nutrition to low-income mothers-to-be. The lack of timely prenatal care and inadequate nutrition are important causes of low birth weight, which is a major contributor to infant mortality. Perhaps for these reasons, the decline in infant mortality slowed during the 1980s.

In summary, even though the infant mortality rates for African Americans have decreased significantly in the past 30 years, the absolute racial difference in infant mortality shows no lasting shrinkage. In the case of both males and females, the racial difference in infant mortality rates in 1989-90 accounts for one year of the difference in life expectancy at birth between the entire African American and white populations of Michigan.

Life Expectancy from Ages 1 to 70

As indicated above, the current concept of premature mortality extends beyond infancy. At the same time, the amount of lifetime lost by failing to postpone death must diminish with age. There is, after all, a maximum of 69 years of potential life between ages 1 and 70. The lifetime lost through premature deaths (i.e. deaths before age 70) is greater for someone who is young (e.g. 10 years of age) than for someone who is older (e.g. 68 years of age).

Taking the preceding into account, a better understanding of the lifetime implications of premature mortality can be obtained by considering the potential years of life expectancy that a population loses by failing to postpone to age 70 those deaths that occur in the 1-70 age range. Moreover, since the prevalence of specific causes of death also varies by age, it is instructive to consider the impact that postponement of specific causes of death would have on the expected years of survival in this age range.[13]

Currently, African American males in Michigan who survive infancy can be expected to live, on average, slightly over 60 of the next 69 years (Table 3). Put otherwise, deaths between ages 1-70 result in a loss of 8.8 years of the potential life expectancy to age 70. White males, by comparison, are expected to live an average of nearly 65 years, representing a loss of just over 4 years of the potential life expectancy between exact ages 1-70. Among females, the losses of potential life expectancy in this age range are 4.75 years for African Americans as compared to 2.5 years for whites (Table 4). Thus, the lost potential is about twice as great for African Americans as for whites.

The impact of mortality in this age range for black males has actually worsened in the past 30 years in both absolute and relative terms. In 1960 for instance, the estimated loss of life expectancy from deaths between ages 1-70 amounted to 7.5 years. Based on current estimates, that loss has increased by more than a year. Meanwhile the loss of potential life expectancy from premature deaths for the white population declined by more than one year. As a result of the improving situation for whites and the worsening condition for blacks, the racial difference in loss of potential life expectancy between ages 1 and 70 has tripled from 1.5 to 4.5 years.

The principal medical causes of death in this age span which are most responsible for limiting the average lifetime of black males have also shifted over the past several decades (Table 3). In the early 1960s, heart disease, cancer, and injury from accidents (in that order) were the three specific causes of death between ages 1-70 that had the most adverse impact on the average lifetime of black males. Postponing deaths from heart disease just within this age range had the potential of increasing the lifetime of the entire black male population by an average of 1.9 years. By comparison, postponing death from homicides would have added a little over 6 months.

Currently, homicides, heart disease, and cancer are, in order of importance, the specific causes of death between ages 1-70 that have the most adverse impact on the average lifetime of black males. Postponing premature deaths from homicides would presently increase the average lifetime among all black males by over 2 years, while postponing deaths from heart disease would lead to a potential improvement of 1.6 years. The adverse impact on average lifetime attributable directly to death from cirrhosis is also more pronounced at present than it was in the early 1960s. Almost half a year could be added to the average lifetime of the entire black male population by postponing deaths from cirrhosis between ages 1 and 70. As a principal cause of death, diabetes registered a relatively small toll on life expectancy between ages 1-70 for black males at the beginning and end of the 30-year period. This probably reflects the fact that diabetes, which is more prevalent among blacks than whites, is more often a contributing rather than a principal cause of death.[14]

Among Michigan's white male population, premature deaths from heart disease, cancer, and accidents are the specific causes of death most responsible for limiting life expectancy from ages 1-70. This was also true three decades ago, although the adverse impact on mortality of white males from these causes of death has generally decreased. In

Table 3.
Components of Loss of Potential Life Expectancy* in Years from Ages 1 to 70 and Apportioned Differences between Black and White Males in Michigan: 1959-61 and 1989-90

	1960*			1990		
	Blacks	Whites	Apportioned Racial Difference	Blacks	Whites	Apportioned Racial Difference
Years of Life Expectancy from Ages 1 to 70	61.54	63.00		60.17	64.74	
Components of Loss of Potential Life Expectancy:						
-Cancer	1.16	1.02	0.14	1.29	0.95	0.38**
-Diabetes	0.13	0.09	0.04	0.19	0.08	0.11
-Heart Disease	1.90	1.97	0.02	1.61	1.02	0.63**
-Cerebrovascular Disease	0.58	0.26	0.28	0.26	0.10	0.15
-Cirrhosis and other Liver Diseases	0.14	0.13	0.01	0.45	0.13	0.31**
-Accidents	0.97	1.16	-0.16	0.71	0.82	-0.06
-Suicides	0.13	0.23	-0.09	0.27	0.33	-0.03
-Homicides	0.57	0.05	0.47**	2.05	0.11	1.85**
-All other causes	1.87	1.07	0.74**	1.99	0.73	1.22**
-Residual	0.05	0.02	-0.01	0.06	0.01	0.0
Total Loss	7.46	6.00	1.46	8.83	4.26	4.57

* There are 69 years of potential life expectancy between ages 1 and 70.

** Contribution to racial difference which is significant at the .05 level.

a) Estimates for 1959-61 are based on data for the population of non-white males in Michigan from ages 1 to 70, of whom 97 percent were Black.

particular, the potential gain from postponing deaths from heart disease has decreased from two years to one year. This reflects the decline over the past several decades of mortality rates for this particular cause of death to white males under age 70.

It is apparent that the causes of death structuring racial differences in mortality have shifted in the past 30 years. Then as now, homicides took a much heavier toll on life expectancy at ages 1-70 among the black male as compared to the white male population, although that gap has widened over time. Now, unlike then, heart disease, cancer, and cirrhosis have emerged to exact much heavier losses in life expectancy among the black males as compared to the white males from ages 1-70.

A general pattern of decline in premature mortality between ages 1-70 among females appears to be accompanied by a decrease in racial differences in average years survived in that age interval. The average years of survival over this age range for African American females increased by 1.5 years—from under 63 years in 1960, to over 64 years in 1990 (Table 4). The improvement for white females amounted to about one year, thus reducing the racial difference in average years of survival between ages 1-70 by about one-half year.

Currently cancer, heart disease, and homicides are, in order of importance, the specific causes of death between ages 1-70 that have the most adverse impact on the longevity of the African American female population. Postponing until age 70 the deaths from either cancer or heart disease would add at least one year to the lives of all black females between ages 1-70, while postponing deaths from homicides would add about one-half a year. Compared to 30 years ago, the lifetime effects of premature mortality from heart disease and strokes have diminished, while the impact of cancer has remained about the same. Distressingly, homicidal deaths appear to be playing a greater role in limiting life expectancy of African American females in this age range.

For white females, the major specific cause of death that limits the life expectancy between ages 1-70 is cancer. Its cost to life expectancy between ages 1-70 appears to have declined by only 0.2 year over the past three decades. Nevertheless, a lack of change among black females during the past 30 years made cancer emerge as a major cause of racial differences in female mortality from ages 1-70.

Despite a decline in the racial difference, the average number of years survived between ages 1-70 is still greater for white than for African American females. Besides cancer, the two causes of premature

Table 4.
Components of Loss of Potential Life Expectancy* in Years from Ages 1 to 70 and Apportioned
Differences between Black and White Females in Michigan: 1959-61 and 1989-90

	1960ᵃ			1990		
	Blacks	Whites	Apportioned Racial Difference	Blacks	Whites	Apportioned Racial Difference
Years of Life Expectancy from Ages 1 to 70	62.72	65.56		64.25	66.50	
Components of Loss of Potential Life Expectancy:						
-Cancer	1.15	1.12	0.19	1.13	0.92	0.25**
-Diabetes	0.23	0.11	0.11	0.18	0.07	0.10
-Heart Disease	1.57	0.69	0.85**	0.98	0.40	0.57**
-Cerebrovascular Disease	0.69	0.24	0.43**	0.26	0.10	0.16
-Cirrhosis and other Liver Diseases	0.12	0.08	0.04	0.18	0.06	0.12
-Accidents	0.37	0.37	0.02	0.35	0.34	0.02
-Suicides	0.04	0.08	-0.04	0.06	0.08	-0.01
-Homicides	0.20	0.03	0.17	0.46	0.05	0.40**
-All other causes	1.91	0.82	1.07**	1.14	0.49	0.64**
-Residual	0.03	0.00	-0.02	0.01	0.00	0.00
Total Loss	6.28	3.44	2.84	4.75	2.50	2.25

* There are 69 years of potential life expectancy between ages 1 and 70.

** Contribution to racial difference which is significant at the .05 level.

a) Estimates for 1959-61 are based on data for the population of non-white females in Michigan from ages 1 to 70, of whom 97 percent were Black.

death that contribute the most to that racial difference are heart disease and homicides. The racial differences attributable to heart disease seem, however, to have diminished since 1960, and significant differences in this age range that were previously attributable to strokes have also disappeared.

Premature death from homicides is the second largest specific cause of death contributing to female racial differences in life expectancy between ages 1-70. The cost to life from homicides rose about one-quarter of a year for black females at ages 1-70, but remained almost constant for white females. Thus, the trends with respect to homicides present a less hopeful image than do those for heart disease and strokes.

MORTALITY AT THE OLDER AGES

The disadvantages in mortality that blacks experience diminish and ultimately disappear at the oldest ages. Racial differences in rates of dying at specific ages become smaller for those surviving throughout adulthood. It has been observed that eventually an age is reached at which whites are dying at a higher rate than are blacks of a similar age.[15] This reversal of differences or "crossover" in mortality rates, however, occurs fairly late in life.

For both males and females, Table 5 shows that the age at which the racial crossover in mortality occurs has advanced over the last 30 years. In 1959-61, the crossover was around 70 years of age in the case of males and close to 74 years in the case of females. In 1989-90 the racial crossover of mortality rates occurs at 79 years of age for males and almost 80 years of age for females.

One of the consequences of the crossover in the rates of mortality at or above age 70 has been that blacks surviving to age 70 are expected to live longer on average than their white counterparts. But even this advantage has disappeared as the racial crossover moves to older and older ages. Table 6 shows that over the past 30 years, the remaining life expectancy for persons reaching age 70 rose more steadily for the older white population, both male and female, than for the older black population. The racial gap in remaining life expectancy at age 70 favored blacks in 1959-61 to the extent of about nine-tenths of a year (i.e., 10 to 11 months). That small edge has disappeared and white males in 1989-90 appear to have about a one-half year advantage over black males at this older age. Similarly for females, the life expectancy at age 70 favored black females in 1959-

Table 5.
Age of Mortality Crossover by Gender, Race, and Period of
Observation for Michigan Residents

Subgroup	1959-61[a]	1969-71[a]	1979-81	1989-90
Black and White Males	70.7	72.0	77.1	79.2
Black and White Females	73.8	73.1	78.8	79.9

[a] Estimates for the black population in these two periods are based on available data for the nonwhite population, during which time over 90 percent of the nonwhite residents of Michigan aged 70 and older were black.

Table 6.
Remaining Years of Life Expectancy at Age 70 by Gender, Race, and
Period of Observation for Michigan Residents

Subgroup	1959-61[a]	1969-71[a]	1979-81	1989-90
Males				
Blacks	10.86	11.79	11.34	11.54
Whites	9.97	10.40	11.13	12.10
Difference	0.89	1.39	0.21	-0.56
Females				
Blacks	13.35	16.83	15.35	15.70
Whites	12.56	13.87	15.15	15.80
Difference	0.79	2.96	0.20	-0.10

[a] Estimates for the black population in these two periods are based on available data for the nonwhite population, during which time over 90 percent of the nonwhite residents of Michigan aged 70 and older were black.

61 by a modest eight-tenths of a year; but in 1989-90, it favored white females by one-tenth of a year. Thus, as the age at which the racial crossover in mortality occurs has increased, blacks have lost the small advantage in remaining life expectancy at age 70 which they once held relative to whites.

IV. POLICY OPTIONS

IMPLICATIONS OF TRENDS IN AFRICAN AMERICAN MORTALITY IN MICHIGAN

As noted at the outset, mortality is an indicator of the health and well-being of a population. Understanding racial differences in mortality conditions does not, in and of itself, dictate precise policies. Rather, knowledge of racial differences in mortality conditions should help to frame discussion of public policy options aimed at equitably providing for the general welfare of the population. In this regard, the trends noted in this study have implications for policymakers as they debate public policy priorities.

First, policymakers need to be aware that the greater burden of mortality on blacks is an enduring problem in Michigan, which in several respects has grown worse over the last 30 years. While national-level racial differences in life expectancy from birth have generally declined, racial differences in Michigan have been increasing. The African American male population in Michigan has experienced no lasting improvement in life expectancy at birth for over a quarter of a century, and the average years of life between ages 1-70 has actually decreased. The African American female population in Michigan has fared better with substantial increases in life expectancy. Here too, however, the racial difference in life expectancy has increased slightly. And while the infant mortality rate has declined substantially, racial differences have not.

Second, policymakers need to recognize that racial differences in life expectancy are the result of a variety of causes of death that vary in etiology. Those making the most significant contribution to differing life expectancies between blacks and whites, for instance, include infant mortality, homicides, heart disease, cancer, and, in the case of males, cirrhosis and liver disease. The policy implication is that it is too simplistic to assume that the problem can be adequately addressed in a single program. The diversity in causes of death that contribute to the racial difference in life expectancy argues for a multifaceted response. Indeed, this appears to be consistent with the view of Michigan's Office of Minority Health, which incorporates each of the five preceding causes of death within its list of eight top health priorities.

Third, policymakers need to be attuned to the complex pattern of age and cause-specific shifts in the character of mortality in the

African American population and how these changes differ for the white population. While the impacts of some causes of death have diminished, others have remained constant or increased. The latter features are evident in the persistent loss in life expectancy for blacks from cancer, and a growing loss in life expectancy, particularly for black males, from homicides and cirrhosis. The medical causes of racial differences in mortality are likely to continue to change. Public health research, for example, indicates that the AIDS case rate in Michigan in the late 1980s was almost five times greater for blacks as compared to whites. Given the high probability of mortality associated with AIDS, it is conceivable that AIDS-related deaths could emerge as yet another important contributor to the lower life expectancy of African Americans. Michigan's Office of Minority Health has incorporated AIDS into its list of top health priorities.

MONITORING, PREVENTION, AND EARLY DETECTION

From a policy perspective, the changing medical causes of mortality and their impact on African Americans highlights the need to support systematic monitoring of health conditions and evaluation of programs aimed at improving health conditions. Establishment of the Office of Minority Health in the late 1980s represented a step in that direction. Whether this office and the Department of Public Health, more generally, are to be successful in these essential tasks will depend on continuity of sufficient levels of state support.

The development of appropriate policy responses to health problems generally is based on an assessment of the factors that place people at risk and the construction of intervention strategies which address those risk factors. The set of relevant risk factors pertaining to the various causes of death may include biological, psychological, or sociological conditions. While the specifics of strategies for dealing with particular causes of death may vary, policies that provide for prevention or early detection and treatment of injuries, diseases, and other health problems deserve high priority. Policies based on these strategies may not only benefit the individuals involved but also reduce the direct and indirect social costs of health.[16]

An important proviso, however, is that the higher mortality among African Americans is in large part also a consequence of relative economic disadvantage. Studies measuring the exact impact of socioeconomic inequality on racial differences in mortality are limited[17] and require further research. Yet it is generally understood that socioeconomic disadvantages of African Americans (as reflected in lower levels of education, income, and access to health care along with higher levels of unemployment) represent critical social risk factors. The implication is that preventive programs alone may not have the desired effect if such social risk factors that contribute to higher mortality of African Americans are not also addressed. Keeping these points in mind, it is useful to reflect on some potential policy responses to those causes of death which contribute most to racial differences in mortality.

Infant Mortality

The capacity to reduce infant mortality provides an example of the benefits of preventive strategies. Low birth weight, a major factor in infant mortality, can be reduced by adequate maternal nutrition and prenatal care. Two federally funded programs pursuing these complementary goals are the Women, Infants, and Children (WIC) program and Medicaid. WIC issues coupons for cereal, juice, milk, and cheese to women who are pregnant, breast-feeding, or less than six months postpartum, and to children aged under five years if they are medically "at risk" and at or below 185 percent of the federal income poverty line. Likewise, Medicaid was created to increase the access of poor people to medical care. However, individual states determine eligibility rules for Medicaid; and in Michigan, only persons whose household income is no more than 65 percent of the federal income-poverty line have qualified for Medicaid. Since the importance of this program has been recognized in providing pre- and postnatal care to women and in reducing infant mortality, the Michigan legislature provided funds in 1987, allowing women at all income levels below the poverty line to become eligible for Medicaid.[18] This initiative anticipated a new federal law that went into effect in July, 1990, *requiring* states to provide prenatal care to all indigent women, regardless of how far below the poverty line they fall.[19] The advantage of such a program is that the cost of prenatal care to prevent low birth weight is less than the cost of providing neonatal intensive care.[20]

Another strategy for reducing infant mortality is to reduce or postpone childbirth among females who are at high risk—such as young teenagers—of experiencing the death of their child. While family planning programs provide a mechanism for encouraging the postponement of childbearing, these programs have suffered a lack of government support in recent years due to controversies over the role that abortion should play in relation to family planning. Thus, the potential of family planning has not been fully implemented with respect to postponing teen-aged childbearing as a means of reducing infant mortality. One of the arguments for postponement is a presumed long-run economic benefit for the mother; but young African American teens might reasonably question the extent to which they can reap those economic benefits. In short, while preventive programs should receive support for addressing the problems of higher infant mortality among African Americans, policymakers should not neglect solutions to systemic problems, such as the lack of economic opportunity.

Homicides

Rather than treating homicides as strictly a law enforcement issue, public health officials and other leaders now recognize that this and other forms of violence are legitimate public health concerns.[21] Homicides involve a complex set of risk factors pertaining to both the victim and the perpetrator. A variety of social risk factors has been argued to contribute to homicides and other forms of intentional injury. Some of these include the prevalence of firearms, alcohol and drug abuse, poverty and joblessness, and portrayal of violence in the media. Psychological factors involved in the learning of violence as an appropriate response for dealing with conflict and stress represent some of the other risk factors.

In reviewing the evidence on these risk factors as it pertains to the health of African Americans, analysts at the National Research Council concluded that: "At present there are no scientifically proven efficacious interventions that would lead to the reduction of homicide. Under the circumstances, limiting access to handguns and training in conflict resolution have been recommended."[22] They also note that acknowledging that the subject of violence is a legitimate public health concern represents an important step in responding to the problem of homicides.

Cirrhosis

Substance abuse in the form of excessive drinking or alcoholism plays a major role in deaths from cirrhosis. The National Research Council[23] notes that both genetic and social factors play an important role in alcoholism; that is, transmission of alcoholism involves both a biological and a learning component. The council noted that further research was needed to provide a sound scientific basis for the development of preventive strategies.

Meanwhile, some concern has been directed to the role of the mass media in promoting alcohol consumption, particularly to those advertising campaigns targeting minority populations. Developing programs to address the problem of alcoholism should be given a high priority among public health officials because it is also a factor in the rate of intentional injuries (e.g. homicides) as well as unintentional injuries (e.g., motor vehicle accidents).

Heart Disease and Cancer

Prevention, early detection, and treatment have been gaining increasing attention in dealing with chronic medical causes of death, such as heart disease and cancer. With the emergence in Michigan of a greater mortality impact of these diseases on blacks as compared to whites during the past 30 years, public health officials should consider the various lifestyle, socioeconomic, and biological characteristics that place blacks at greater risk of dying from these diseases.

black males, for instance, are more likely to smoke than white males and are thus at greater risk of heart disease, although black females are not more likely to smoke than white females. National surveys show that obesity and hypertension are more prevalent among African American males and females than among whites.[24] Obesity has been identified as a risk factor for diabetes.[25] If not always the principal cause of death, diabetes and hypertension are often contributing factors to mortality from cardiovascular disease.[26]

Data from the Michigan Cancer Surveillance Program show that in 1990, the single most common site of malignant tumors among black and white Michiganian males was the prostate gland, and national estimates indicate that this form of cancer increased 61 percent between 1973-88.[27] It is not understood why black males have a higher incidence rate, but it has been speculated that a higher-fat diet, earlier age at initiation of sexual activity, and possibly earlier infection with venereal disease may be important reasons.[28] Blacks tend to be diagnosed at a more advanced stage of the disease, and this partially accounts for their higher death rate from this cause. But it is unknown why blacks are more likely than whites to die from prostate cancer even when the stage of the disease at initial diagnosis is the same.[29] One study suggested that education was a more important factor than race in the survival of prostate cancer.[30]

The next most common sites of malignant tumors in Michiganian males, black and white, are the lung and bronchus,[31] a major cause being tobacco smoke. A survey in Michigan in the early 1980s showed that blacks were more likely to smoke than whites and that the racial difference had widened. The growing gap was not due to the greater tendency of blacks to start smoking (the proportions in this category were almost the same for blacks and whites) but the lesser tendency of blacks to quit smoking.[32]

Among women, breast cancer was the leading primary site for diagnosis of malignancy at ages 25 or over.[33] From 1970-83, death rates from breast cancer in Michigan were very similar for black and white women; but after 1983, black women began to evidence an increase while white women stayed the same.[34] Some reasons for this trend are that blacks are less knowledgeable about the warning signs of cancer and about the administration of breast self-examinations and are more pessimistic about their ability to survive cancer.[35] These characteristics may delay black women from seeking diagnosis of cancer at an early stage. Thus, the invention and institutionalization of mammography as a standard procedure in annual checkups for high-risk women have perhaps advantaged white women relative to blacks. These relationships suggest that the higher death rate of black women from breast cancer is sensitive to their lower average level of educational attainment.

V. CONCLUSIONS

In recent times, the American electorate has been encouraged to ask whether they are better off now than four years ago as a means of evaluating the effectiveness of public policies and the success of public officials who are responsible for those policies. This review of racial differences in mortality in Michigan asks whether the African American population is better off now than it was in 1960. Although one could argue that the evidence provides a mixed response to this question, the essential point is that after three decades there are several respects in which it is not. While the policy options for addressing the specific causes of death that contribute to this situation include programs of prevention along with early detection and treatment, it is important to remember that without changes in fundamental economic disadvantages the success of such programs may be limited. How Michigan's policymakers will respond in the closing decade of this century remains to be seen.

ACKNOWLEDGMENTS

The data analysis was conducted when Dr. Christenson was a Research Fellow and Dr. Johnson was a Visiting Scholar at the Population Studies Center of the University of Michigan. We thank Cheryl Anderson-Small, Joe Darden, Reynolds Farley, William Frey, Albert Hermalin, Kathy Humphrys, Rose Maria Li, Brendan Mullan, Lisa Neidert, Jeffrey Passel, Gregory Robinson, Anne Santiago, Jeffrey Taylor, Lauralee Thompson, Ching-li Wang, and Lindy Williams for constructive discussions. We are grateful to the Institute for Public Policy and Social Research of Michigan State University for purchasing our usage of the unit record tapes on the 1989 and 1990 death certificates for Michigan. The authors retain sole responsibility for analyses and interpretations.

NOTES

1. Richard G. Rogers, "Living and Dying in the USA: Sociodemographic Determinants of Death among Blacks and Whites," *Demography* 29, no. 2 (1992): 287-303; National Research Council, *A Common Destiny: Blacks and American Society* (Washington, D.C.: National Academy Press, 1989); Verna M. Keith and David P. Smith, "The Current Differential in Black and White Life Expectancy," *Demography* 25, no. 4 (1988): 625-32.
2. Initial estimates of the overall or crude death rates for 1989-90 indicate approximately 9.9 deaths per 1,000 African American males. But the crude rates obscure the real extent of white males' advantage in mortality by not taking into account the fact that whites are on average older than blacks. Since one generally expects higher levels of mortality at older ages, a more appropriate measure of comparison is one which is adjusted for differences in the age composition of the groups being compared. When the age composition of blacks is made comparable to that of whites, the African American death rate increases to 12.8 deaths per 1,000 individuals. This "age standardized" rate represents a level of dying that is 46 percent higher than that of white males. Although the racial differences are somewhat less for females, an age standardized comparison of the two populations shows that the overall level of mortality is still 27 percent higher for black as compared to white females.
3. Several technical points are worth noting regarding the calculation for life expectancies. First, in order to avoid anomalous single-year fluctuations, which might distort more enduring changes in mortality, life expectancy and the other measures of mortality in this report are an average of the recorded deaths to Michigan residents for three-year intervals surrounding each census (e.g. 1959-1961, 1969-1971, and 1979-1981). In the case of the most recent census date, the information on deaths is averaged for the

two-year (1989-1990) period since the data for 1991 were not available in time for this analysis. Second, as death records during the 1959-61 and 1969-1971 periods did not distinguish blacks from other minority races, the information for these years includes the entire non-white population. However, since blacks constituted at least 95 percent of the non-white population in Michigan during these periods, the data should accurately reflect mortality conditions of the state's African American population at those time periods. (While the authors are confident that the data on non-whites provide an accurate portrayal of the mortality situation of blacks during the early 1960s and 1970s, it would not be appropriate to make this assumption for subsequent time periods, because the non-white population has become increasingly heterogenous: about 88 percent African American in 1980, and 85 percent in 1990.) Finally, in the calculations on which this report is based, national-level estimates of undercounting have been used to adjust the census data for the state to more accurately reflect the true population counts (Siegel 1974). The calculations of mortality reported herein for 1989-90 are based on the assumption that the undercounts in the 1990 census are similar to those in the 1980 census.

4. Reynolds Farley and Walter R. Allen, *The Color Line and the Quality of Life in America* (New York: Oxford University Press, 1989).
5. Ibid.
6. National Center for Health Statistics, *Vital Statistics of the United States, 1988, Volumn II, Mortality, Part A* (Washington, DC: U.S. Government Printing Office, 1991).
7. Farley and Allen, *The Color Line.*
8. Ibid.
9. National Center for Health Statistics, *Vital Statistics.*
10. J.C. Kleinman, "Mortality," *Statistical Notes for Health Planners, National Center for Health Statistics* (February 1977): 1-16; Janet D. Perloff, Susan A. LeBailly, Phillip R. Kletke, Peter R. Budetti, and John P. Connelly, "Premature Death in the United States: Years of Life Lost and Health Priorities." *Journal of Public Health Policy* 5, no. 2 (1984): 167-84; J.M. Romeder and J.R. McWhinnie, "Potential Years of Life Lost between Ages 1 and 70: An Indicator of Premature Mortality for Health Planning." *International Journal of Epidemiology* 6 (1977): 143-51.
11. Christiane B. Hale, "Infant Mortality: An American Tragedy," *Population Trends and Public Policy* 18 (1990): 1-17.
12. In 1959-1961 and 1969-1971, non-white births and deaths were not tallied separately for blacks versus other peoples of color by the Michigan Department of Public Health. However, black females of childbearing ages (15-44) represented 97.36 percent of all women of color in this age range in the 1960 Census of Michigan, and 94.52 percent in 1970. Therefore, we have used the non-white infant mortality rates as estimates of the black infant mortality rates for these two time periods.
13. Multiple decrement life tables and the techniques for apportioning of deaths from specific causes are discussed in Chiang (1984), Keyfitz (1985), Namboodiri and Suchindran (1987), Smith (1988 and 1992), and Pollard, et al. (1990).

14. Kenneth G. Manton, Clifford H. Patrick, and Katrina W. Johnson, "Health Differentials between Blacks and Whites: Recent Trends in Mortality and Morbidity," *The Milbank Quarterly* 65 (supplement 1 1987): 129-99.
15. Kenneth G. Manton and Eric Stallard. *Recent Trends in Mortality Analysis.* (Orlando, FL: Academic Press, 1984); Kenneth G. Manton, Sharon Sandomirsky Poss, and Steven Wing, "The Black/White Mortality Crossover: Investigation from the Perspective of the Components of Aging," *The Gerontologist* 19, no.3 (1979): 291-300.
16. Hale, "Infant Mortality."
17. Rodgers, "Living and Dying in the USA."
18. Michigan Department of Public Health, *Minority Health in Michigan: Closing the Gap* (Lansing: Michigan Department of Health, 1988).
19. Hale, "Infant Mortality."
20. Ibid.
21. Michigan Department of Public Health, *Minority Health in Michigan*; National Research Council, *A Common Destiny.*
22. National Research Council, *A Common Destiny.*
23. Ibid.
24. U.S. Department of Health and Human Services, *Blood Pressure Levels and Hypertension in Persons Aged 6-74 Years: United States 1976-80* (Hyatsville, MD: U.S. Public Health Service, 1982); U.S. Department of Public Health and Human Services, *Health, United States, 1991* (Hyatsville, MD: U.S. Public Health Service, 1992).
25. Farley and Allen, *The Color Line.*
26. Manton, Patrick, and Johnson, "Health Differentials."
27. Janet T. Eyster, Peter J. DeGuire, and Georgia H. Spivak, *Cancer Incidence and Mortality: Michigan 1990* (Lansing: Michigan Department of Public Health, 1992).
28. Ibid.; Manton, Patrick, and Johnson, "Health Differentials"; Michigan Department of Public Health, *Minority Health in Michigan.*
29. Eyster, DeGuire, and Spivak, *Cancer Incidence and Mortality: 1990.*
30. H.H. Dayal, L. Polissar, and S. Dahlberg, "Race, Socioeconomic Status, and Other Prognostic Factors for Survival from Prostate Cancer," *Journal of the National Cancer Institute* 74 (1985): 1001-6.
31. Eyster, DeGuire, and Spivak, *Cancer Incidence and Mortality: 1990.*
32. Michigan Department of Public Health, *Minority Health in Michigan.*
33. Eyster, DeGuire, and Spivak, *Cancer Incidence and Mortality: 1990;* Janet T. Eyster, Peter J. DeGuire, Georgia H. Spivak, and Berhanu Alemayehu, *Cancer Incidence and Mortality: Michigan 1989* (Lansing: Michigan Department of Public Health, 1991).
34. Eyster, DeGuire, Spivak, and Alemayehu, *Cancer Incidence and Mortality: 1989.*
35. Manton, Patrick, and Johnson, "Health Differentials."

REFERENCES

Chiang, Chin Long. 1984. *The Life Table and Its Applications*. Malabar, FL: Robert E. Krieger Publishing Company.

Dayal, H.H., L. Polissar, and S. Dahlberg. 1985. "Race, Socioeconomic Status, and Other Prognostic Factors for Survival from Prostate Cancer." *Journal of the National Cancer Institute* 74: 1001-6.

Eyster, Janet T., Peter J. DeGuire, and Georgia H. Spivak. 1992. *Cancer Incidence and Mortality: Michigan 1990*. Lansing: Michigan Department of Public Health.

Eyster, Janet T., Peter J. DeGuire, Georgia H. Spivak, and Berhanu Alemayehu. 1991. *Cancer Incidence and Mortality: Michigan 1989*. Lansing: Michigan Department of Public Health.

Farley, Reynolds and Walter R. Allen. 1989. *The Color Line and the Quality of Life in America*. New York: Oxford University Press.

Hale, Christiane B. 1990. "Infant Mortality: An American Tragedy." *Population Trends and Public Policy* 18: 1-17.

Keith, Verna M., and David P. Smith. 1988. "The Current Differential in Black and White Life Expectancy." *Demography* 25 (4): 625-32.

Keyfitz, Nathan. 1985. *Applied Mathematical Demography*, 2d ed. New York: Springer-Verlag.

Kleinman, J. C. 1977. "Mortality." *Statistical Notes for Health Planners*, National Center for Health Statistics (Feb.): 1-16.

Manton, Kenneth G., and Eric Stallard. 1984. *Recent Trends in Mortality Analysis*. Orlando, FL: Academic Press.

Manton, Kenneth G., Sharon Sandomirsky Poss, and Steven Wing. 1979. "The Black/White Mortality Crossover: Investigation from the Perspective of the Components of Aging." *The Gerontologist* 19(3): 291-300.

Manton, Kenneth G., Clifford H. Patrick, and Katrina W. Johnson. 1987. "Health Differentials between Blacks and Whites: Recent Trends in Mortality and Morbidity." *The Milbank Quarterly* 65 (supplement 1): 129-99.

Michigan Department of Public Health. 1988. *Minority Health in Michigan: Closing the Gap*. Lansing.

____.1982. "Infant Deaths in Michigan: Analysis and Recommendations." Unpublished manuscript. Lansing.

Namboodiri, Krishnan, and C. M. Suchindran. 1987. *Life Table Techniques and Their Applications*. Orlando, FL: Academic Press.

National Center for Health Statistics. 1988. *Vital Statistics of the United States, 1991, Volume 2, Mortality, Part A*. Washington, DC: U.S. Government Printing Office.

National Research Council. 1989. *A Common Destiny: Blacks and American Society*. Washington, D.C.: National Academy Press.

Perloff, Janet D., Susan A. LeBailly, Philip R. Kletke, Peter R. Budetti, and John P. Connelly. 1984. "Premature Death in the United States: Years of Life Lost and Health Priorities." *Journal of Public Health Policy* 5 (2): 167-84.

Pollard, A. H., Farhat Yusuf, and G. N. Pollard. 1990. *Demographic Techniques*, 3d. ed. Sydney: Pergamon Press.

Rogers, Richard G. 1992. "Living and Dying in the USA: Sociodemographic Determinants of Death among Blacks and Whites. *Demography* 29 (2): 287-303.

Romeder, J. M., and J. R. McWhinnie. 1977. "Potential Years of Life Lost between Ages 1 and 70: An Indicator of Premature Mortality for Health Planning." *International Journal of Epidemiology* 6: 143-51.

Siegel, Jacob. 1974. "Estimates of Coverage of the Population by Sex, Race, and Age in the 1970 Census." *Demography* 11: 1-23.

Smith, David P. 1988. *User's Guide for Program SURVIVAL*. Houston, TX: University of Texas School of Public Health, Houston.

____. 1992. *Formal Demography*. New York: Plenum Press.

U.S. Department of Health and Human Services. 1982. *Blood Pressure Levels and Hypertension in Persons Aged 6-74 Years: United States, 1976-80*. Hyattsville, MD: U.S. Public Health Service.

U.S. Department of Health and Human Services. 1992. *Health, United States, 1991*. Hyattsville, MD: U.S. Public Health Service.

II.
Employment Policy
for Michigan

Worker Training in Michigan: A Framework for Public Policy

Joel Cutcher-Gershenfeld and Kevin J. Ford

I. INTRODUCTION

Job training is an important strategic lever for building a highly skilled workforce that simultaneously commands high wages and increases the competitiveness of the firm.[1] From a policy perspective, though, there is controversy in Michigan and elsewhere as to the appropriate role of the state in facilitating the building of a highly skilled workforce. Underlying the controversy are complex philosophical issues, as well as practical problems with coordination and integration—all of which limit the ability of Michigan's public and private training initiatives to realize their full potential.

The extent to which current practice in the private and public sectors fall short of what is possible, calls for a closer examination of the issues relevant to job training. While many public and private training initiatives do compare favorably with initiatives in other states, the appropriate points of comparison are at the same time both more local and more global in nature. A local focus within Michigan shows that there is a large variation in program access and policy innovation. From a global perspective, there are alternative models for worker training in Germany, Japan, and other nations that demand serious consideration and debate.

To facilitate dialogue about worker training, this article presents a stakeholder framework for addressing training policy. By identifying the various stakeholders with strong underlying interests or concerns about workplace training, it is possible to compare current practices with the potential range of practices. It is also possible to identify important issues that emerge from this analysis which can, in turn, help structure the debate regarding training policy. Among the relevant stakeholders are elected political leaders, state and local government staff responsible for training programs, employed and unemployed workers, youths about to enter the workforce, current public and private sector employers, prospective employers, and local communities.

The stakeholder framework leads to a number of specific policy recommendations, which are presented in as non-partisan a fashion as possible. Maintaining a non-partisan tone is not easy. Training is a highly visible policy issue in which specific initiatives have become associated with the current or past governors of the state. Also, training is taking on increased priority under the Clinton administration, which may add a further partisan overlay to the issue. We hope the stakeholder framework is useful in fostering an issue-driven dialogue about worker training in Michigan that recognizes and then rises above partisan concerns.

II. STATEMENT OF THE PROBLEM

The problems with worker training in Michigan are multi-fold. Some of the problems are structural in nature, such as centralization but, at the same time, fragmentation of programs, constraints on access by individuals and employers, and the lack of mechanisms to identify and diffuse innovations. Other problems are political and ideological in nature, including prevailing business ideologies that focus on cost-cutting competitive strategies and the politicization of training initiatives. Ultimately, the problem (and the solution) lies in the overlapping and competing interests of the multiple stakeholders with concerns about worker training in Michigan. Each of these issues are discussed in turn.

CENTRALIZATION AND FRAGMENTATION OF PROGRAMS

State and federal training programs (administered through state agencies) involve millions of dollars of training expenditures. In general, public training funds can be used to upgrade skills of employed individuals, retrain dislocated workers, and provide job skills for the unemployed. In fact, the state and federal programs vary according to the direct recipients of training funds, the administrators of the funds, the sources of the training funds, and the focus of the training. Table 1 provides an overview of selected training programs in Michigan, with information on these various dimensions.

A large number of state-financed programs have been eliminated under the Engler administration, centralizing state activity around a few major federal programs and a handful of remaining state programs. The Federal Job Training Partnership Act (JTPA), which is administered through the Michigan Department of Labor, represents the largest amount of funding for training in the state (between $400 and $500 million). These funds are based on Title II and focus on job retraining for dislocated workers and skill training for the disadvantaged. A second source of federal money for training includes two programs—Employers Designing Gainful Employment (EDGE) and MOST—that emphasize building employable skills for welfare recipients. Both programs are administered by the Department of Social Services.

The largest state-funded training program is the Adult Alternative Training Grant, which is funded through the Department of Education and jointly administered by the Departments of Commerce, Education, and Labor, and the Michigan Employment Services Commission. The grants, which totaled 25 million in 1992, are given to community colleges and other vocational training centers with state accreditation to develop customized training programs for area employers. Other state programs, such as the Community Development Block Grant from the Commerce Department, set aside a small amount of money for job training to support businesses that facilitate economic development by encouraging job growth. In the past, substantial state training dollars were also devoted to economic attraction and job creation grants to employers considering expansion in Michigan. It is unclear how much money is still being utilized for these purposes since there is no longer a formal program structure for such funding.

The analysis of funding indicates that a large proportion of training dollars is from federal grants that focus on dislocated workers, the unemployed, and welfare recipients. A relatively small amount of state funding focuses on the development and administration of

Table 1.
Descriptive Information on Selected Worker Training Programs in Michigan

Program Name	Direct Recipients of Funding	Level of Funding in FY 92	Sources of Funding	Types of Training Supported
Job Training Partnership Act	Displaced Workers and the Unemployed	$400 - $500 Million	Federal Grant (Title II) (Channeled through State Department of Labor)	Job Skills
Employers Designing Gainful Employment (EDGE); MOST	ADC/Welfare Recipients	$1 - $2 Million	Federal Grant (Channeled through State Department of Social Services)	Initial Job Skills
Adult Alternative Training Fund	Community Colleges and other Accredited Facilities	$25 Million	State (Department of Education)	Employee Upgrade Training
Community Development Block Grants	Small Businesses	Variable	State (Commerce Department)	Job Training for New Employees

training programs for improving business competitiveness through the enhancement of employee skills. For example, public training programs are not oriented toward supporting organizational and individual development in areas such as team-based work systems, group problem-solving, communications, and strategic planning— despite the fact that these developmental training topics are essential to the effective utilization of technical training.[2] Also, most of the worker training is oriented to retraining dislocated workers, with only a limited number of apprenticeships and other school-to-work transition programs. This state of affairs contrasts sharply with Germany, Sweden, and many other nations that boast near-comprehensive, one- or two-year skills training programs for non-college bound youth.

The federal and state funds are administered by a variety of state agencies. The four programs illustrated in Table 1, for example, involve four separate state agencies. Additionally, at the local levels, there are Private Industry Councils (PICs) and Economic Development Councils (EDCs) that have primary responsibility for administering various training funds. Each state agency and local administrative unit has its own internal culture and operates within its own policies and procedures. As a result, the status of training and the administration of the respective training programs varies. For example, worker training is not the primary focus of the state Department of Education, while it is the reason for the creation of PICs. At the same time, even if worker training is not central in the Department of Education, the training programs in this department benefit from access to a statewide network of secondary schools and community colleges. In contrast, the PICs have had to establish their legitimacy and build a set of networks with existing institutions in the communities.

Taken together, then, public training programs in Michigan are at once centralized (i.e., large programs administered by a few departments or state agencies) and fragmented (a proliferation of various training initiatives and delivery systems). In addition, the range of the targeted audience is primarily limited to the dislocated and unemployed with a heavy reliance on federal grants for sources of funding for training.

Two additional administrative bodies should be noted—one for its absence in the administration of training programs, and the other for programs administered independently from the government. The first is the federal government, which had played a low-profile role over the past dozen years in terms of direct program administration—though this is already changing under the Clinton administration. The second administrative source is the private sector, which includes private employers, private vendors, unions and joint union-management training efforts. Private sector training accounts for the majority of training that does occur (though there are few exact estimates of the proportions).[3] The training activities in private sector are addressed at various points in this chapter as they are relevant to policy formulation and implementation.

CONSTRAINTS ON ACCESS BY INDIVIDUALS AND EMPLOYERS

The movement in the state to limit the focus of training grants has led to a discontinuity of programs that are most relevant to employers through the upgrading skills of employees. This reflects, in part, the lack of consensus as to what the role of the state should be relative to building a highly skilled work force. In recent years there have been two attempts to simplify matters—one technological and the other organizational. Both, however, have proven vulnerable to political shifts.

The technological change was termed the "Opportunity Card," which was a "smart card" that ultimately would be issued to all citizens in Michigan. The cards would contain personal profile information and allow individuals to discover programs appropriate for people with profiles such as theirs. The cards have been criticized as requiring an unwieldy support system of data, ATMs, etc., and the concept, which originated under a Republican governor, has now become ideologically identified with the past Democratic governor. As a result, the initiative has been halted, leaving access to training programs for individuals a matter of either luck or great perseverance.

The organizational change involved the establishment of the Governor's Office for Job Training (GOJT), which was intended to provide a centralized coordination mechanism—especially for training funds for active workers channeled through employers. With the last change in administration, however, the GOJT was criticized as representing too much of a concentration of power and many of its functions were disbanded or parceled out to other state agencies. Both experiences reveal the degree to which administrative structures and programmatic solutions can be vulnerable to political change (an issue addressed more fully below), but they also represent what seems to be movement away from a policy commitment toward facilitating client access to public programs.

In addition, individuals and employers are sometimes denied access to certain kinds of funds. For example, training funds included as part of economic development inducement packages are generally limited to outside employers intending to relocate in Michigan or to Michigan employers intending to build new facilities. This can create equity problems for long-established Michigan employers who are direct competitors with the firms receiving the state aid. The long-established firms can essentially say, "we have been paying taxes in Michigan for decades and now you use those dollars to subsidize our direct competitors." This problem is particularly acute in the auto supply industry where great efforts are often made to attract Japanese parts suppliers, yet we already have a large base of U.S. auto parts suppliers in Michigan.

FEW MECHANISMS FOR IDENTIFYING AND DIFFUSING INNOVATIONS

There are innovations in worker training to be found throughout the State of Michigan. Many of the innovations feature public-private partnerships, which is a concept that has received both Republican and Democratic support. Yet, there is no systematic mechanism or set of mechanisms for identifying and diffusing the innovations.

For example, one Muskegon employer—Anderson Pattern—approached its local community college regarding the establishment of various courses in metalworking and other skills relevant to its employees. Using Quick Start funds from the Department of Education, the community college was able to develop the required courses. Within a short period of time, the number of courses being taken by Anderson Pattern employees approached the course load of a two-year degree. Further conversations between the college and the employer resulted in some employees taking the additional distribution requirements (such as English) and thus being awarded a customized degree. Based on this success, the college approached other area employers and subsequently established customized degree programs for them as well. Such customized degrees are being awarded by other community colleges around the state as a result of similar case-by-case interactions with local employers. There is not, however, an appropriate way to evaluate such emergent innovations and facilitate the diffusion of positive lessons.

A similar story can be told about dozens of partnerships being forged by employers and local school districts. The focus of these partnerships is on the school-to-work transition. The partnerships reflect employer interest in a skilled work force and school interest in job opportunities for its graduates. Though great value is emerging from many of these arrangements, there are also anecdotal stories of great frustration on the part of either employers or school districts. With evaluation and assistance, the innovative models could be more easily diffused and all parties might gain.

PREVAILING BUSINESS IDEOLOGY FOCUSED ON COST CUTTING COMPETITIVE RESPONSES

U.S. firms are facing unprecedented domestic and international competition. The dominant response has been to downsize their work forces and otherwise cut costs. While many firms utilize the rhetoric of quality, only a few (e.g., Xerox, Motorola, and Ford) have oriented their competitive responses around adding value through quality. Scholars such as Magaziner and Reich[4] have been critical of U. S. firms given the capacity of many other nations to compete against the United States on the basis of cost. The distinction is particularly relevant in the area of training. Where a business strategy is focused on just being a low cost producer, investment in training is likely to be constrained. In contrast, where a business strategy is focused on being a high value-added producer, investment in human resources will be viewed as essential to business success.

There are two key policy implications relevant to this distinction among business strategies. First, publicly supported training programs may be less likely to achieve their full potential if the firms involved are primarily focused on cutting costs. The support for training in such cases is not likely to lead to enduring change. Recent research on government support for training has found that the programs do not replace existing training activities (which address a long-standing critique of government funding for training), but that the new training programs do not persist once grant funds are used up.[5] Second, there is a clear public interest in better understanding the social costs of alternative business strategies. While cost cutting as a competitive response may make sense to each individual firm, the overall impact is detrimental to the social fabric.

Given that the link between training and business strategies is poorly understood and that this link is central to the effectiveness of public training programs, the controversial implication is that government has a legitimate public interest in the business strategies of firms.

POLITICIZATION OF POLICY INITIATIVES

Michigan's current and prior governors have taken diametrically opposite approaches to worker training. Jim Blanchard, the prior governor, made training a centerpiece of his efforts to stimulate the economy and invested heavily in technology and organizational vehicles to better coordinate training. John Engler, Michigan's current governor, campaigned against such programs as representing an inappropriate utilization of government resources. As a result, training programs have taken on a political dimension.

Some degree of politicization of training may be unavoidable given the ideological splits in this country regarding the appropriate size and role of government. Unfortunately, the consequences of such splits are quite severe. Bold, far-reaching programs are placed at great risk, yet it is just such programs that have the greatest prospect of transforming the way training occurs in this country. In other nations that feature comprehensive training programs, such as Germany or Sweden, the core features of these programs are not subject to debate—reflecting their centrality to the lives of most citizens.

MULTIPLE STAKEHOLDERS WITH OVERLAPPING AND COMPETING INTERESTS

Ultimately, the picture that emerges from our analysis is one where training programs feature multiple stakeholders with both overlapping and competing interests. The stakeholders span both public and private sectors. From this diversity comes innovation and a capacity to serve many audiences, but the diversity also brings confusion and turf battles.

Broadly speaking, the challenge for policymakers in Michigan (and elsewhere) is twofold. First, where there are common interests, it is important that policymakers be creative in identifying and helping to pursue those common concerns. Second, where there is conflict, it is important that policymakers be skilled in surfacing and resolving the conflicts, rather than leaving them to fester. The following policy recommendations are crafted with these two broad goals in mind.

III. KEY POLICY ISSUES

To help frame debate on training policy, we have identified four broad topic areas where core assumptions have not been fully surfaced or debated. In each case, the focus is not on advocating particular policies or programs. Rather, the material is presented so that policymakers, employers, and individual citizens might reassess the limitations associated with the present structure of public debate and action on training.

RECOGNIZING THE PUBLIC CONSEQUENCES OF PRIVATE BUSINESS AND INDIVIDUAL CAREER DECISIONS

As deTouqueville[6] observed more than 100 years ago, American culture tilts heavily toward individualism without a sufficiently counterbalancing concern with collectivism. Consequently, we protect individual managerial prerogatives and the rights of workers to manage their own careers—even when the outcomes may not be beneficial for either party or society.

In regard to job training, it is usually viewed as a managerial prerogative whether or not to offer training to employees. Thus, there is great resistance to notions of a mandated commitment of a certain percentage of payroll costs to training. Advisors of President Clinton have mentioned a 1.5 percent requirement, which is much less than the 3 percent requirements in Germany, Holland, and other European communities.[7]

Similarly, there is resistance to the one- or two-year apprenticeships common in many European nations. They are seen as too intrusive a form of tracking for our youth. Yet, the individualism and entrepreneurial spirit that we are ostensibly fostering, too often becomes a well-protected freedom to fail. Most Americans would quickly reject the notion that government has a legitimate role in dictating the business strategies of firms, yet, it is also clear that short-term cost-cutting strategies by firms have great effects on local communities and the state.

There is much to debate regarding the costs and benefits of particular programs that force employer investment in training; structure entry into the workforce for our youth; or mandate long-term, value-added business strategies. The broader issue, for policymakers, however, is to examine underlying assumptions regarding the necessary autonomy of firms and individuals when it comes to decisions on training. There is increasing evidence to suggest that the individual decisions of firms and workers are generating sub-optimal outcomes given rising competitiveness at the regional, national, and global levels. Thus, the initial framing of public policy on training must involve full debate and attention to the degree of legitimate government interest in the private decisions of firms and individuals regarding training.

We believe that government has a legitimate role in asserting the collective interests of society, but the available language and ideological frameworks are inadequate for the task. The debates are usually cast in black-and-white terms—either government should have full responsibility, or there should be no governmental influence present. Asserting collective interests in this area requires a more subtle array of options. Government can be positioned as a facilitator, as a source of seed funding, as an information source, as a partner, as a specialist, and (to use Teddy Roosevelt's term) as the "bully pulpit." The challenge is to orchestrate these many possible roles—all of which are likely to be at play in different areas of training—mindful that each represents an assertion by the government that some type of intervention can lead to beneficial outcomes for the state that would not be obtained if these domains were left solely to private firms and individual workers.

RECOGNIZING THE PRIVATE CONSEQUENCES OF PUBLIC POLITICAL DECISIONS

There was a time when key governmental functions (such as public welfare or unemployment insurance) had private-sector counterparts that were of equal or greater significance in the particular areas of service provision. During the course of the twentieth century, however, many private vehicles for charity and insurance have been largely or completely replaced by federal, state, and local government.

Training, however, still remains an area where there is substantial activity within government and, concurrently, within the private sector—without clear criteria for distinguishing what should be public and what should be left to private sector firms or individuals. As a result, new public training initiatives, abandonment of existing initiatives, and specific administrative practices by government all have deep consequences for the training choices of firms and individuals.

When new government training programs are announced, firms and individuals will assess the value added associated with the programs.

There are usually costs (at least in terms of time) in taking advantage of government funded training programs, so the public initiatives are weighed against available private sector alternatives. When a decision is made to view the government (including state agencies, community colleges, secondary schools, etc.) as a preferred provider for certain kinds of training, much of the training infrastructure (classrooms, materials, qualified instructors, etc.) is left to government. Thus, for example, secondary schools are increasingly core providers of workplace literacy training. Community colleges are taking on similar core roles in generalized technical skills, such as blueprint reading or pneumatic principles.

It is not clear, however, that government agencies fully appreciate the degree to which these areas of distinctive competence also carry the responsibility of assuring quality and continuity. There are no well-established procedures for evaluating the extent to which the training programs developed are effective in meeting employee and employer needs. In addition, there are no mechanisms to assure firms or individuals that programs begun in partnership between private and public sectors will continue to be provided. In fact, the public sector has a reputation for beginning and abandoning programs—for ideological, turf, or budgetary reasons. Thus, it is critical that policymakers fully recognize and attend to the implications for the private sector relevant to public policy decisions.

BALANCING THE NEED FOR MANY SERVICE DELIVERY MECHANISMS AGAINST THE REQUIREMENTS OF EQUITY AND ACCESS

In the structure and delivery of training, government is faced with a core strategic choice. On the one hand, there is a natural tendency toward multiple service delivery mechanisms—reflecting the many state and local agencies and institutions involved in training. At the same time, government has a responsibility to assure firms and individuals that there is an equitable basis for the distribution of these public goods, including some measure of equal access. Firms and individuals understand that every training program and initiative can not be made available to every interested recipient, but they are angered by the degree to which the process is seen as unfair, inaccessible, or just incomprehensible.

Both Republican and Democratic leaders have recently decried the confusing array of over seventy public training programs at state and local levels.[8] Yet little is being done to remedy the situation. There is plenty of room for legitimate debate over what types of training government should provide and what roles it should play in the provision of training. None of this debate is possible, however, without full information on the existing array of programs, the specific way in which they are structured, and the ways in which they are perceived by the private sector and the local community.

In this arena, as in many others, perception quickly becomes reality. Currently, the perception (and probably the reality) is that the array of governmental programs is complicated and that access varies considerably by individuals' characteristics, governmental agency, region of the state, and type of program. Thus, regardless of any particular policymaker's view on how much training should be provided by government, it is important that all government officials recognize the need for strategic planning and coordination of what is being provided.

One key complicating factor associated with the planning and coordination of public training activities is the often greater lack of coordination and planning around training in the private sector. Both survey research and case studies of private training[9] point to a very limited integration between training activities and business planning in firms. Anecdotal conversations with corporate managers responsible for the training function highlight a lack of even the most rudimentary estimates regarding how many people are being trained in what mix of technical and developmental skills. As such, it is difficult to assess what is or is not occurring in the private sector and, thus, what the implications are for public sector planning.

PROMOTING A CONTINUOUS LEARNING ORIENTATION IN WORKPLACES THAT SERVES SOCIETAL AS WELL AS BUSINESS NEEDS

Despite the overall lack of coordination and integration in the private sector, there are selected firms that are truly exemplars for developing a workplace culture oriented to continuous learning—where training becomes integral to business strategies and competitive success. Below are three examples of Michigan firms in which training innovations have helped to build work force skills and maintain high-wage jobs, as well as to increase the competitiveness of firms.[10] Thus, the training provides value-added on societal as well as business dimensions.

Weyerhaeuser Structurwood, located in Grayling, Michigan, is a customer-driven particle board manufacturing facility within a larger paper and wood products corporation. The plant balances high-volume production with value-added flexibility in product specifications. Work is organized around a team system with workers being paid based on the number of jobs they know how to do (pay-for-knowledge), rather than one particular job they happen to be performing. The plant has become the corporate benchmark for training and work organization in a medium-sized facility. One key innovation in training practices in this new start-up facility is the development of an extensive train-the-trainer and peer appraisal system, both of which are instrumental in the development of a continuous learning orientation within the work teams.

National Steel/USWA, located in Ecorse, Michigan, is a large integrated steel-making facility under joint U.S. and Japanese ownership. In order to compete in the world marketplace, the firm has made massive investments in new technology and worked with the Steelworkers Union to construct what they call a "cooperative labor-management partnership." Integral to the partnership are employment security guarantees made by the firm in exchange for a reduction in job classifications and the establishment of cross-training programs for skilled trades.

Buick City/UAW, located in Flint, Michigan, is proud to produce one of the few U.S. vehicles to rank among the top quality cars on the J.D. Powers survey. The plant is organized on a team-based system, which was implemented within an existing facility. Extensive training opportunities have been developed under a joint, union-management structure in order to implement the team system and to later add a full second shift of operations. The focus of training at Buick City has been directed to production workers.

These are just three examples of training innovations in Michigan firms. Other unionized and nonunion firms in this state are also moving toward the integration of continuous learning systems with business operations. These experiences suggest that promoting continuous learning among firms is consistent with goals of developing a highly skilled work force in Michigan, with relatively high wages, and enhancing firm competitiveness.

ESTABLISHING EFFECTIVE VEHICLES FOR JOINT, PUBLIC-PRIVATE GOVERNANCE

The analysis above suggests that private decisions about training have important public consequences, and public decisions about training have important private consequences. Given that the mix of public and private programs is generally uncoordinated and poorly integrated, the stage is set for serious exploration of appropriate public-private partnership structures for the governance of training activities. There is a great deal of discussion these days regarding public-private partnerships, but neither practitioners nor policymakers have much guidance regarding the establishment and operation of such arrangements. Public-private partnerships surface core questions, such as:

- What decisions can public officials cede to public-private forums without abandoning their public responsibilities?
- What decisions can private organizations cede to public-private forums without abandoning their responsibilities to stockholders, union members, and other constituents?
- How can appropriate voice be given to key parties that are not well organized, such as youths that are about to enter the work force, or the unemployed?

The answers to these and other pressing questions cannot be completely found in existing experiments with public-private partnerships. The highly varied experience with Private Industry Councils (PICs) and with employer-school partnerships suggests that partnerships can be either quite effective or can prove to be highly unsatisfactory. To help set the stage for a more systematic process to answer questions about public-private partnerships, Table 2 lists the interests of key stakeholders regarding key aspects of the governance of training. Any discussion of partnerships must be rooted in a clear understanding of the common and competing interests that potential partners bring to the relationship.

Across one dimension, Table 2 distinguishes among three major stakeholder groups—government, employers, and individuals.[11] By government, we are referring to elected state officials, state civil service employees (including program administrators), and local/county government officials. Included among employers are both current and prospective employers. Individuals include active employees (who may or may not be represented by a union), the unemployed,

Table 2.
A Comparative Assessment of the Interests of Government,
Employers, and Workers in Training Initiatives

	GOVERNMENT	EMPLOYERS	INDIVIDUALS
THE AMOUNT AND DIRECTION OF PUBLIC FUNDS DEVOTED TO TRAINING	Effective spending of scarce resources (for example, avoiding substitution effects) Targeting training dollars to increase the competitiveness of firms and the standards of living of citizens	Responsible management of tax dollars (for example: avoiding unfair subsidies to competitors) Public funds focused on "general" skills to avoid "free rider" costs associated with employees being hired by employers who do not provide training	Appropriate balance in spending on training for the unemployed, employed workers, and youths entering the work force Links between training programs and career/labor market opportunities
THE AMOUNT AND DIRECTION OF PRIVATE FUNDS DEVOTED TO TRAINING	For employers to take a long-term, developmental approach to employment relations (to minimize the burden on government retraining programs)	Getting the most value for training dollars spent Balancing training costs against investment in technology, hiring employees who already have needed skills, and other business development strategies Focusing training dollars on "firm specific" skills to reduce turnover and increase competitiveness	Opportunities to receive skill upgrading and career development training Opportunities to apply new skills and knowledge Equity in the administration of training
THE ESTABLISHMENT OF PUBLIC PRIVATE PARTNERSHIPS	Multiplying the effectiveness of public dollars spent on training Direct input into decision making Ensuring that partnerships help meet government policy objectives (for example: equity, targeted sectors for growth, etc.)	Multiplying the effectiveness of private dollars spent on training Direct input into decision-making Ensuring that partnerships help meet strategic business objectives	Some form of input into decision making Increased training opportunities as a result of the partnership

and youths about to enter the work force. Where appropriate, the entries in Table 2 reflect the diversity within each stakeholder group.

Across the second dimension of Table 2, we highlight three key issues relevant to public-private partnerships. First, we examine stakeholder interests regarding the expenditure of public money on training. Second, we examine stakeholder interests regarding the expenditure of private money on training. Finally, we examine stakeholder interests regarding the administration and operation of public-private partnerships themselves.

A close look at Table 2 reveals many areas of overlapping or common interests among the three major stakeholder groups. All parties have a shared interest in the effective spending of both public and private training dollars. Both government and employers approach the idea of public-private partnerships with many of the same concerns about decision making and other aspects of the governance of such initiatives. These and other areas of commonality represent important building blocks for the creation of public-private partnerships.

There are also a number of areas where the interests of the key stakeholders are different, but complementary. For example, the government prefers to spend training dollars on general skills so that the "return on the investment" will accrue over a citizen's lifetime, regardless of where they work. At the same time, firms prefer to invest in firm-specific training both to achieve high returns for the firm and to minimize lost investment as a result of turnover. Similarly, workers prefer some form of input into the direction and delivery of training, while employers want to ensure that the training is delivered in a way that is effective and directly usable. Though the interests of the parties are different in each of these examples, they complement one another in both cases. In discussing public-private partnerships, it is critical to recognize domains where the pursuit of separate and distinct priorities can generate joint gain.

Finally, there are some areas where the interests of the stakeholders are in conflict. For example, employers are attempting to strike an effective balance between investment in training and alternatives to training such as outside hiring or importing new technology. Where the decision is made not to invest in training, it will conflict with employee interests in increasing employer investment in development of human resources. Similarly, the government is interested in utilizing training investments to increase job growth, which may result in greater investments for growing firms and less investment for stable firms—a direct conflict with a concern among firms that government investment not provide some firms with an unfair competitive advantage over others. Given that it is inevitable that there will be instances where there are conflicts of interest, it becomes critical that public-private partnerships establish mechanisms to surface and resolve these sources of conflict.

It is important to note that the form of any public-private partnership can vary widely. In some cases, it is limited to a bilateral relationship between a firm and a community college or secondary school. More challenging, and potentially further reaching, are emerging partnerships that involve multiple parties—including secondary schools, community colleges, vocational centers, universities, manufacturing employers, service and retail sector employers, and private training service providers. Sometimes these are established as regional consortia or as industry-based consortia. For example, the Grand Rapids Employers Association includes 200-300 businesses that coordinate training needs and program administration in order to gain economies of scale while preventing unnecessary duplication. A key policy issue concerns the appropriate roles of state and local government in such partnerships.

IV. SUMMARY AND CONCLUSIONS

Training is increasingly viewed as central to the competitive success of Michigan's firms and to the career growth and development of Michigan's citizens. While the potential impact of training initiatives is large, the current reality is a tangled mix of programs and initiatives in public and private sectors that is poorly documented, not well integrated, and a target for ideological battles. Untangling the situation will not be easy.

The point of departure lies in a thoughtful assessment of the legitimate interests that the public sector has regarding the decisions of firms and individuals, as well as a parallel assessment of the legitimate interests that firms and individuals have regarding the structure and operation of public sector initiatives. Public-private partnerships provide one avenue for mutual benefit, though an assessment of the multiple interests at play helps to explain the limited success to date with such partnerships.

To realize the full potential gain possible from public-private partnerships, the same principles of continuous learning that some private sector firms are applying to their internal operations might well be applied to this key area of public policy. Continuous learning depends on mechanisms for feedback, monitoring, coordination, and multi-party decision making. It implies a shared approach to program administration that is simultaneously focused on broad goals and attentive to program details. If these concepts were explicitly built into public-private partnerships and general public policy on training, it would become possible to conceive of a state where the individual, private efforts of firms, the public efforts of government, and the joint public-private initiatives were all rooted in a common language and philosophy—which would surely have far-reaching implications for meeting the broad goals of business, society, and government.

NOTES

1. Anthony Carnavalle, *America and the New Economy: The New Competitive Standards are Radically Changing American Workplaces* (San Francisco: Jossey-Bass, 1991). Also see reports from the Commission on the Skills of the American Workforce, *America's Choice: High Skills or Low Wages* (Washington, D.C.: National Center on Education and the Economy, 1990) and the Cuomo Commission on Trade and Competitiveness, *The Cuomo Commission Report.* (New York: Simon & Schuster, 1988).

2. The link between technical and developmental training is more fully developed in Kevin Ford and Joel Cutcher-Gershenfeld, *Rethinking Workplace Training: A Stakeholder Approach to Improving Practice and Public Policy* (New York: Oxford University Press, forthcoming).

3. It is difficult to estimate the full scope of training activity since so much training occurs as on-the-job (OJT) training, which is rarely documented.

4. Ira Magaziner and Robert Reich, *Minding America's Business: The Decline and Rise of the American Economy.* (New York: Harcourt Brace Jonavich, 1982).

5. Harry Holzer, Richard Block and Jack Knott, "Do Training Subsidies Matter? State Subsidized Training in Michigan Firms," *ILR Review* 46, no. 4 (July 1993): 625-36.

6. Alexis de Tocqueville, *Democracy in America,* (London: Longman, Green, Longman & Roberts, 1862).

7. Magaziner and Reich, *Minding America's Business.*

8. Comments at IPPSR conference on "Reinventing Government," 7 December 1992. Lansing, MI. Note that a number of the seventy programs mentioned are initiatives under the JTPA which we have treated as a single program.

9. See case findings in Ford and Cutcher-Gershenfeld, *Rethinking Workplace Training;* and survey research by Kevin Ford on the link between business planning and training practice.

10. These examples are all from Ford and Cutcher-Gershenfeld, *Rethinking Workplace Training.*

11. These three stakeholder groups where highlighted by John Dunlop, *Industrial Relations Systems* (New York: Holt Reinhardt, 1958) as the three key actors in any industrial relations system.

Workers Compensation in Michigan: A Disabled Disability System?

Karen Roberts

I. STATEMENT OF THE PROBLEM

Workers' compensation is one of the oldest forms of social insurance in the nation. The enabling legislation in Michigan, Public Act 10, was enacted in 1912. The social contract underlying workers' compensation rests upon a bargain struck between employers and workers, where workers received a guarantee of prompt medical care and partial replacement of lost wages in exchange for freeing their employers from the fear and cost of defending against tort claims for nearly all work-related injuries and illnesses. This creation of an insurance-based rather than tort-based system was expected to minimize the need for legal disputes. At the time of this original bargain, the concept of disability was limited to that resulting from traumatic, one-time, usually accidental, workplace injuries. With a few exceptions, recovery was expected, as was return to work.

Two important trends in the work place are on a collision course in the context of workers' compensation. The first is the changing nature of the employment relationship. The restructuring of the economy, evidenced by the continued trend toward "right-sizing" and the rise of contingent employment (the use of temporary, part-time, and/or leased employees), is changing the nature of work and the basic relationship between employers and workers. The second trend is the changing nature of workplace injury. An increasing share of these injuries are being attributed to repetitive motion, cumulative trauma, and stress. These cases tend to be long term, of ambiguous cause, and difficult to diagnose, with little consensus about treatment and degree of recovery.

For most workplace injuries, which create what are called temporary total disabilities, the original workers' compensation bargain is adequate. Individuals have an accident at work, make a claim, receive wage loss benefits and medical care, and return to work. The serious problems that plague workers' compensation and threaten its ability to function do not occur with every claim, but rather arise with the more complex injuries.

While complex injury cases were always troublesome, the increasing use of contingent workers and decline of what was an implicit long-term employment relationship is forcing a difficult issue. Employers who are becoming increasingly unwilling and unable to make long-term commitments to able-bodied employees are equally, if not more, unwilling to guarantee long-term income to those who no longer work for them due to a disability.

The basic premise advanced in this chapter is that most of the serious problems confronting workers' compensation arise out of this conflict between the changing nature of work and the changing nature of workplace injury. From this perspective, most of the specific policy problems related to workers' compensation can be seen as evidence of the strains this conflict is imposing on the original workers' compensation bargain. *The fundamental policy issue for workers' compensation is whether the original bargain between employers and workers is sufficiently resilient to adapt successfully to these new demands or whether a new bargain must be struck.*

Part 2 of this chapter elaborates on this fundamental policy challenge facing workers' compensation. Part 3 provides a review of what experts cite as the most serious problems facing workers' compensation programs both in Michigan and the nation.[1] This discussion is organized around two policy areas: 1) the need to balance the costs and benefits of the workers' compensation system; and 2) issues of program administration and the need for due process. It will become clear in this discussion that most of these problems arise with the more complex types of injuries. The common theme threaded though the discussion of each programmatic issue is that any durable policy solutions must recognize and respond to the fundamental policy challenge to workers' compensation presented by the changing employment relationship.

In 1984, Professor Theodore St. Antoine submitted to then-governor James Blanchard a comprehensive evaluation of the state of workers' compensation in Michigan. Included in the introduction to that report was a list of pressing issues for workers' compensation; H. Allan Hunt in his 1979 monograph noted that these same issues had been cited in a 1962 speech by William Hart, then director of the Michigan Workmen's Compensation Department. Hunt observed that most of Hart's comments remained relevant in 1979; and St. Antoine noted that most of both Hart's and Hunt's observations continued to speak to the condition of workers' compensation in 1984. To only slightly misquote Professor St. Antoine, "As we shall see, the observations of both Hart and Hunt [and St. Antoine] retain much force in [1993]."[2]

II. THE FUTURE OF WORKERS' COMPENSATION: IS IT VIABLE IN ITS PRESENT FORM?

It is often said that the problems of workers' compensation could best be addressed if the two stakeholders for whom the program was designed—employers and employees—were to meet and discuss and structure reforms without input from the cast of what should be more peripheral characters (government, insurance carriers, health care providers, attorneys, and rehabilitation providers). There is clearly wisdom in this suggestion because most of the success stories in workers' compensation occur when employers and employees work together. However, this apocryphal discussion between employers and employees would have to take place in the context of what may be the most profound change in the new employment relationship—right-sizing and the rise of the contingent work force.

The contingent work force refers to those segments of the labor market where employment is part time or temporary. Although these work arrangements have always existed, both have grown substantially over the last decade. Table 1 shows the growth patterns between 1980 and 1988. Most analysts expect this trend to continue as employers restructure their operations, move to leaner organizational structures, increasingly rely on subcontracting, and reduce their permanent work forces. The long-term employment relationship—where workers are employed by a single employer for much of their working lives—is thus becoming less common.

This work force restructuring presents problems to workers' compensation. For most injuries that are the result of traumatic accidents, treatment is clear and recovery is relatively certain. These injuries do not strain the original workers' compensation contract nor do they pose problems for the new employment relationship. The tension arises when the cause of injury is not clear-cut and results in a long-term disability where the degree of incapacity is difficult to determine unambiguously, such as with repetitive motion injuries.

One hallmark of repetitive motion injuries is that while a worker may recover sufficiently to resume normal activities, returning to the old job, or one like it, often invites reinjury. Once the expectation of a full recovery and return to the old job is diminished, the logic of constraining workers' compensation to a contract between an individual employee and his/her employer is challenged. This raises the question of whether or not, under what is supposed to be a no-fault system, individual employers should be responsible for possible long-term income maintenance and/or significant rehabilitation and training costs for a worker who is injured in their employ.

The answer provided by the workers' compensation statute is "yes."[3] But, as the number of complex cases increases and the basic employment relationship between worker and employer is weakening across the economy, this answer is less clear. This problem was alluded to by Professor St. Antoine in his report when he suggested that it is possible that workers' compensation may not be equipped to handle certain types of disabilities.[4] One indication that many employers throughout the nation are changing their answer to "no" is the increasing levels of dispute in workers' compensation.[5]

Attorney involvement is a frequently named culprit in the rising dispute level. However, the inherent conflict in the two trends cited earlier—a decrease in long-term employment and an increase in more complex injuries—may be the root cause. Increased litigation over workers' compensation may be more of a symptom than a problem. If so, reducing attorney involvement will not, by itself, improve the functioning of the workers' compensation system. *If the basic problem is that the scope of the challenges facing workers' compensation exceeds the range of the original bargain, then the policy challenge will be to redesign the social contract in such a way that the rights of injured workers are protected and the state's employers bear their fair share of the costs.*

III. KEY POLICY ISSUES

While the objectives of workers' compensation are fairly straightforward, there are some inherent tensions that complicate its implementation: the tension between workers' compensation as social insurance providing adequate income replacement to the disabled worker and as a cost of doing business for the employer; and the tension between the need to guarantee due process for both employers and employees, balanced against a need for efficient and low-cost program administration. In practical terms, these tensions create a number of specific problems for policymakers in Michigan and in other states. These issues include:

A. Costs and Benefits of the System
- Defining disability: Deciding who is, and who is not, eligible for benefits
- The effectiveness of medical cost containment: Controlling health care costs without limiting access to quality treatment
- The adequacy of indemnity benefits: Providing adequate income replacement
- The status of open competition and the future of the Accident Fund of Michigan

B. Administration of the Program
- Minimizing delays and backlogs in the dispute resolution system
- Financing the Bureau of Worker's Disability Compensation and ensuring mediation and rehabilitation services

The background and current state of each of these issues will be discussed along with relevant policy initiatives enacted or being considered in other states as well as how each issue relates to the question of the role of workers' compensation in the emergent employment relationship.

A. COSTS AND BENEFITS

Definition of Disability

Deciding on the appropriate definition of disability has plagued workers' compensation since its inception. The difficulty arises out of the nature of disability as a medical problem embedded in a labor market context.[6] In the simplest case, a worker is injured on the job, becomes temporarily disabled from doing that job, but eventually recovers and returns to work. This picture becomes complicated when the disability is long term or permanent, and the nature of the disability moves from what was primarily a medical question to one of ability to work.

States vary in how they handle this problem. Michigan is a "wage-loss" state, meaning that disability is defined in terms of lost earnings.[7] Other state systems also include impairment benefits. Under an impairment system, the degree of physical impairment is evaluated at the point maximum healing is deemed to have occurred, and the injured worker is compensated by a lump sum payment to the degree there is a residual physical limitation, even if the person is fully capable of performing his/her previous occupation. This type of benefit award entails what can be an elaborate and conflict-ridden evaluation process, which Michigan avoids under its current wage-loss system.[8]

Use of a wage-loss system places Michigan's benefit system firmly in the context of prevailing labor market conditions. Under the Michigan system, benefits can be terminated if an employee "receives a bona fide offer of reasonable employment. . .and. . .refuses that employment without good and reasonable cause" (ML 418.401.3[a]). Reasonable employment is defined as "work that is within the employee's capacity to perform . . . that is within a reasonable distance from that employee's residence. . .[and] shall not be limited to work suitable to his or her qualifications and training" (ML 418.401.7).

In Michigan, injured workers receive 80 percent of after-tax lost wages. If an injured worker returns to a job paying less than the pre-injury wage, benefits are equal to 80 percent of the difference between the two after-tax weekly wages. These provisions have been operationalized with reference to an actual job offer. If a person returns to a lower-wage job, the benefit calculation is based on actual post-injury earnings. If a person returns to the same or a better-paying job, benefits stop. Clearly, the better economic conditions are, the easier it will be for an individual to find a job.

A recent decision by the Michigan Court of Appeals, *Sabotka v Chrysler Corp.*, challenges this link between the definition of disability and labor market conditions.[9] The thrust of this ruling is to shift the definition of wage loss from the difference between pre-injury wages and *actual* post-injury wages to the difference between pre-injury wages and what the worker *could* earn. In other words, the availability of an actual job is no longer a prerequisite for establishing wage loss (the basis for benefits).[10]

One likely result of this ruling is to move Michigan closer to an impairment system. In order to establish what someone can earn without reference to a specific job offer, some type of assessment of physical abilities will have to be conducted. Impairment rating processes have not been trouble-free in other states. In fact, these impairment assessment procedures have been the focal point of litigation. So, any gains in this sort of move would have to be balanced against the costs.[11]

A more troublesome policy question is how this ruling will affect the original workers' compensation bargain. The definition of disability is rarely an issue for short-term temporary total disabilities and usually only applies to the problematic, complex injury cases discussed earlier. The ruling from *Sabotka v. Chrysler* represents one possible—but inadequate—version of reform of the original bargain of workers' compensation. It has the potential to allow employers to discontinue benefits to injured workers they do not expect to re-employ, but it offers nothing to the injured worker. An adequate restatement of the workers' compensation bargain will have to address both parties' concerns.[12]

Effectiveness of Medical Cost Containment

In the debate over the workers' compensation crisis, one point of agreement is that rising medical costs are an important driver behind the overall increase in workers' compensation costs. In most states, the implementation of cost containment measures in workers' compensation has lagged that in general health care. Part of the reason for the delay is that many cost containment measures potentially conflict with the basic bargain between injured workers and their employers because, one way or another, these measures tend to restrict access to care.[13]

State responses to medical cost increases in workers' compensation have varied. The Michigan response, which took effect in August 1989, provides for a fee schedule that specifies the maximum fee a provider can receive for most medical procedures, and a utilization review process.[14] Within the fee schedule there are a large number of procedures for which a maximum fee is unspecified, and actual payments are negotiated for those procedures on a claim-by-claim basis.

Whether or not the cost containment schedule has reduced costs is not clear. Anecdotal evidence suggests that it has.[15] However, one study, using data on medical costs per claim six months before and six months after the implementation of cost containment, found that costs have not been substantially reduced.[16] Using claims data from a large insurer in the state, this study found that after controlling for the mix of injuries, the median payment per claim increased by $38, or 25.7 percent.[17] After examining the nature of the cases where costs appeared to increase, this study found that providers were shifting either the type of procedures they performed or their description of these procedures into categories that were unspecified by the fee schedule. In addition, it appeared that more cases were meeting the criteria that required state utilization review. The policy conclusions were: (1) the number of procedures unspecified in the fee schedule should be reduced; and (2) the resources devoted to utilization review probably need to be increased.

One concern about the implementation of these measures was that restricting provider payments would reduce injured worker access to good medical care.[18] There is no evidence that deterioration in access to medical care has occurred as a result of cost containment. However, one study using focus groups of injured workers found that being denied medical treatment when workers' compensation was the only source of insurance coverage was common.[19] From the injured worker perspective, the reasons typically given for provider reluctance to treat workers' compensation patients were delays in payments, paperwork, and a higher-than-otherwise likelihood of having to provide medical testimony.

From a policy perspective, it appears that while the implementation of a fee schedule does not seem to have reduced access to medical care, there was a problem with access prior to its implementation that will not be ameliorated by the current cost containment strategy. One solution currently under debate is what is called 24-hour coverage where no distinction is made between work and non-work causes of injury. A version of this has been legislated in Florida where employers are required to purchase a 24-hour coverage health insurance policy, and employees are required to pay any deductibles or copayments specified under that policy. Ontario has 24-hour coverage, and because it is embedded in the Canadian national health system, has no deductibles or copayments. Other states are using deductibles without 24-hour coverage, a measure that is likely to reduce costs but also access. A third measure under consideration is the use of managed care such as PPOs and HMOs. For this to be implemented in Michigan, the existing statutory requirement allowing employee choice of provider after the first ten days would have to be changed. Again, the question of access arises since part of how these systems keep costs down is usually through the use of a referral system beyond basic care.

The issue of medical cost containment is especially salient to any reformulation of the original workers' compensation bargain. Rising medical costs is a major contributor to the escalating costs of workers' compensation. The problem of rising medical costs and society's ability to pay has reached crisis proportions outside of workers' compensation. Employers are increasingly reluctant to foot the medical insurance bill for their employees. Part of the current concern is demographically based: predictions are that our aging population will suffer increasingly expensive illnesses. Workers' compensation has all of these problems but fewer tools to address them. Rising rates of cumulative trauma and repetitive motion injuries mean protracted treatments and higher utilization review costs. Finding ways to equitably distribute these costs will be central to the reformulation of the workers' compensation bargain.

Adequacy of Indemnity Benefits

During periods of fears about the cost of workers' compensation there is usually little discussion over the adequacy of wage-loss benefits. In fact, in at least one state (Massachusetts), the response to rising costs has been to lower the statutory replacement rate. Michigan's statutory benefit rate is 80 percent of after-tax wages up to the maximum of 90 percent of the state average weekly wage. Because Michigan's benefit base is net rather than gross earnings (the base used by all but three other states), a direct comparison of its benefit structure to other states' is difficult. One simulation model concluded that benefits for temporary total disabilities are relatively generous in Michigan and among the most equitable compared to other states.[20]

The benefit adequacy problem arises with long-term disability, and in this matter Michigan is not alone. Of the fifty states and the District of Columbia, only sixteen have provisions for automatic cost-of-living increases in benefits for long-term disabilities. Workers' compensation benefits to Michigan employees who become injured on the job are based on wages at the time of the injury and do not change regardless of how long the disability continues.[21] Using a simulation model, a worker earning $20,000 at the time of injury will see the replacement rate of lost spendable from workers' compensation income fall to 68 percent by year three of the disability, 61 percent by year five, and 45 percent by the tenth year.[22]

During a period when the discussion of the crisis in workers' compensation is primarily phrased in terms of skyrocketing costs, possible plant closures, and potential loss of insurance coverage, the issue of benefit adequacy may not be seen as the most urgent. However, the policy problem remains, even if the current financial climate is inimical to raising the issue.

Under current law (ML 418.364), the office of the director of Bureau of Worker's Disability Compensation (BWDC) is required to do a biannual evaluation of the effects of inflation and other factors on benefit adequacy and present the results to the legislature. Because benefit adequacy is primarily a problem with long-term cases, this issue, also, will become more of a problem as the magnitude of complex injuries increases. Resolution of this problem in the context of the changing employment relationship requires reexamination of the workers' compensation bargain for longer-term-disabilities, not just a simple debate over benefit indexation.

The State of Open Competition in Michigan and the Future of the Accident Fund

Nationally, workers' compensation has become an issue because cost increases are accelerating and seem to be intractable. Most states use an administered pricing system where workers' compensation insurance rates are set by a regulatory body within the state.[23] This rate setting system involves a political balance between the demands of employers who argue for the need to keep costs to a minimum to maintain their economic competitiveness, and insurance carriers who argue that rates must be set high enough to maintain carrier solvency. The rapid increase in costs over the last decade has heightened the tension between these two sets of demands.

According to William Hagar, president of the National Council on Compensation Insurance, insurance carriers are being blamed for the message of rising costs. Hagar and others argue that most state regulators fail to recognize that workers' compensation is no longer a profitable line of business for many carriers.[24] Several states are facing flight by insurance carriers who maintain that they can no longer afford to provide workers' compensation coverage unless they are permitted to increase rates. The most dramatic example is Maine, where there are only two private carriers left.

On the employer side, workers' compensation has risen on the agenda of concerns by private sector managers. In a cross-industry study of 576 employers, conducted by Tillinghast, 30 percent responded that they expected their workers' compensation costs to be out of control over the next five years, and 69 percent responded that these costs were threatening their financial results. Of this same group, 38 percent said that workers' compensation was affecting their decisions about where to locate facilities.[25] There is also the anecdotal but dramatic evidence of firms reducing their work forces or going out of business because of the increases in their workers' compensation costs.[26]

The cost of workers' compensation to employers was an issue in Michigan long before this current well-publicized crisis was facing many other states. Attention turned to how the cost of doing business in Michigan affected its competitiveness, and to workers' compensation as part of that cost. One area of reform was in workers' compensation pricing.

Until 1981, Michigan was an administered pricing state. Initial proposals for reform included a 20 percent across-the-board cut in manual rates.[27] However, the State took a far bolder step and moved to "open competition," so that beginning in January 1983, insurance carriers were required to independently set their own rates, regulated only by the competitive forces of the marketplace.

It is difficult to definitively evaluate the success of this reform, but there are several indications that it has worked well. Two major studies evaluating the effect of open competition in Michigan have been conducted since its implementation.[28] The first found that Michigan employers were paying between 26.3 percent and 30.6 percent less than they would have under the old system, and that between 1978 and 1984, Michigan costs had dropped from 33 1/3 percent above the national average, to 4 percent below. The more recent study indicates that open competition has kept Michigan costs to employers below the national average, however the rate at which costs have dropped has slowed considerably since 1984.[29] Despite insurer complaints that the workers' compensation market is ceasing to be profitable, Michigan has not experienced the exodus of insurance carriers that is occurring in other states.

From this, one might conclude that Michigan has solved its cost problem. However, for several reasons, policymakers cannot be sanguine about the effectiveness of open competition. First is the slight upward trend over the last two years in the share of policies now in the residual market. The residual market, also called the assigned risk pool, is that portion of the market that provides coverage to employers who are denied coverage in the voluntary market. Figure 1 shows

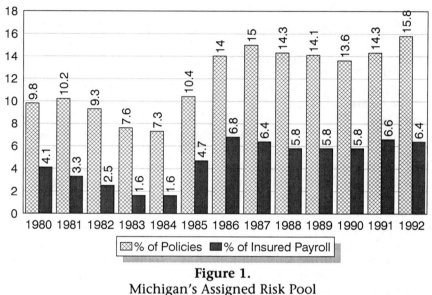

Figure 1.
Michigan's Assigned Risk Pool
% of Policies and Payroll Insured in Work Comp Market

the magnitude of assigned risk coverage in Michigan. The most common reason an insured goes into the residual market is a poor loss history. Increases in the assigned risk pool market share are usually considered a danger sign because they signal a rise in the share of the market viewed by private carriers as an undesirable risk.

The share of business in the assigned risk pool in Michigan is well below the national average (approximately 25 percent), but the recent upturn should be monitored. The policy question is whether this increase in Michigan is due to increasing hazardousness in the workplace or because the secular increases in costs are driving carriers to refuse risks they would have previously accepted. If the latter is the cause, this means that while Michigan appears to be escaping the bitter regulatory struggle over rates, that battle may actually be being silently fought with carriers refusing coverage to high-risk employers rather than raise rates.[30]

An additional policy issue associated with the effectiveness of open competition is the role of the Accident Fund of Michigan. The Accident Fund is a competitive state fund, which means that it is a state agency that functions much like a private insurer: it sets its rates competitively and writes business in the voluntary market (that is, it sells coverage to private-sector employers just like the other insurance carriers in the state). Its market share has grown from 3.9 percent in 1983[31] to 16.9 percent in 1991, down from 18.3 percent in 1990.[32] While many argue that the Accident Fund serves to anchor the competitive market in terms of rates and service, others argue that it operates just like a private carrier but has enjoyed an advantageous tax position that is unfair to the private carriers. Beginning in 1990, the Accident Fund was required to deposit the equivalent of what it would pay in state taxes into a fund to be used for uninsured workers to eliminate its cost advantage related to other carriers. More recently, Governor Engler has proposed the sale of the Accident Fund, arguing that the state should not operate in the private market.

As a legally mandated good, workers' compensation insurance is price-inelastic: short of laying off workers or shutting down business in Michigan, employers have no legal choice about its purchase. Open competition coupled with the self-insurance option *may* be sufficient to keep workers' compensation prices affordable for the state's employers. If not, the question of how the state can best address that problem will remain. Reintroduction of rate regulation is, of course, one solution. But, the presence of a competitive fund as a player in the carrier market may be preferable to regulation.

Again, the best financing scheme for workers' compensation in Michigan will depend on if, and in what ways, the basic bargain is renegotiated. The current system constrains the problem of who bears the costs to the individual employer-employee relationship. This may be an anachronistic arrangement. While there may be clear social benefits to adequate income maintenance, good medical care, and aggressive rehabilitation, disability management and placement, from the point of view of the individual employer against whom a workers' compensation claim is made, these benefits may not justify the costs.

B. ADMINISTRATION OF THE PROGRAM

Delays and Backlogs in the Dispute Resolution System.

The dispute resolution process in Michigan continues to be plagued with backlogs and delays. Peaking at nearly 40,000 cases in 1982, the number of cases pending declined until 1986 when it began to increase, leaving it at just over 31,000 at the end of 1991. Prior to 1986, cases were heard by thirty-nine administrative law judges (ALJs) who were employed through the State Civil Service System. As a result of amendments to the Act in 1985, the ALJs were replaced in 1987 by thirty politically appointed magistrates.[33] Under the 1985 reforms, the magistrates were required to produce written opinions (which contain "findings of fact" and supporting statutory and/or case law citations), in contrast to the prior system where ALJs indicated their decisions by checking a box. Currently, the time between a request for hearing and the actual hearing is about two years (the average for cases heard in 1991 was 705.8 days).[34] Appealing a decision adds up to another year to the process.

Generally, the problem of delays and backlogs in the dispute resolution system is thought to be more of a problem for injured workers than for employers. Once a case reaches the formal dispute resolution system, the employment relationship has usually seriously deteriorated. Workers with disputed claims rarely return to the same employer; and often, benefits are suspended until the case is settled.[35]

However, delays can translate directly into premium increases for employers insured in the voluntary market. The basis for the premium paid by employers insured in the voluntary market is the class code mix of their work force[36] adjusted by an experience modification factor (mod factor) that reflects the individual employer's loss history (a mix of frequency and severity of the claims made against the employer). When insurers incorporate this loss history into the premium, they base it on "incurred" losses, which include reserves, rather than actual losses. *In other words, what employers pay is based on what the insurer thinks a given injury will ultimately cost rather than what it has actually cost so far.* Therefore, in a disputed case, although benefits to the injured worker may be suspended until the dispute is resolved, the reserve reflects the potential costs of the case should the employer lose the dispute. This means that it is not uncommon for an employer to be paying a premium reflecting "losses" or benefits when it is quite possible that only a fraction or perhaps none of those benefits will be paid out to an injured worker. Clearly, the more quickly a case is resolved the more quickly the mod factor can be adjusted to reflect actual losses, frequently leading to a reduction in premium.

One de facto solution to the problem of delays in resolving disputes is the use of redemptions (lump-sum settlements that usually occur prior to a hearing). Redemptions do speed up the process but not by much. The average time between filing a request for a hearing and a redemption award was 512.9 days for redeemed cases that closed during 1991. While redemptions have the advantage of reducing uncertainty, there are some concerns about their adequacy as a substitute for due process. Employers feel that the possibility of a lump-sum payment encourages "nuisance" claims that are without merit but not large enough to pursue through the entire dispute resolution process. Employees often feel that they are being "starved" into accepting an inadequate and unfair settlement.

Numerous reasons are given for the delays in case resolution. One is the variable productivity of the magistrates. During 1991, the range in the number of decisions written by individual magistrates varied from 2 to 106. The conversion of the adjudication board from civil service to political appointment was expected to increase accountability, but the informal consensus among experts in the state is that this has not occurred. Another reason for delays, something of a Catch-22, is that because so many cases are redeemed just before the hearing, magistrates deliberately overfill their dockets, often cannot hear cases at the time originally scheduled, and so postpone them until the next opening—usually months away. A reduction in the number of "courthouse steps" settlements would allow for more realistic scheduling but that reduction is unlikely to occur as long as cases are likely to be postponed.

In 1992, Governor Engler proposed a Ten-Point Program for streamlining the dispute resolution process that has met with mixed reviews. Part of the purpose of his proposal is to increase accountability, measures that potentially could slow the process further. One of the ten points is for the Workers' Compensation Management Committee to study the reasons for the delays and make recommendations, a process that should generate useful policy alternatives.

Improving the efficiency of the dispute resolution process is important to the well-being of both injured workers and the state's employers. As the Michigan work force ages, it is expected that the incidence of more complex claims will increase. Research on the factors that contribute to the likelihood of contesting a claim suggest that claimant uncertainty about future health increases that probability.[37] Using the backlog as an indicator, it is clear that the existing dispute resolution process is not meeting the current needs of the workers' compensation system. If one accepts the basic premise of this chapter, there will be more disputes as employers chafe against the original workers' compensation bargain. An adequately renegotiated bargain should reduce the pressures on the dispute resolution process. Failure to renegotiate spells trouble for what is already an over-taxed dispute resolution system.

Financing the Bureau of Workers' Disability Compensation (BWDC) and Ensuring Mediation and Rehabilitation Services

Unlike some states, such as Ohio, where the program is administered by state government, workers' compensation is a private system in Michigan. Employers purchase insurance coverage from private sector insurance carriers who are responsible for payment of indemnity benefits and medical and rehabilitation costs.[38] The primary roles of government in the Michigan system are oversight and dispute resolution. Currently, the BWDC, the Board of Magistrates, and the Appellate Commission are funded out of general state revenues.[39]

Beginning in 1992, serious discussion began about cutting the workers' compensation budget. Initial proposals made in the spring would have reduced the number of mediators from thirty-two to five and completely eliminated the rehabilitation oversight function. A last minute rescue occurred whereby Safety, Education, and Training (SET) funds were transferred to the Bureau, avoiding mediator layoffs. However, the rehabilitation oversight staff was reduced to one professional and one clerical worker.

The use of SET funds was a one-time solution, and the problem of BWDC funding continues. Although the BWDC performs several functions, the mediation and rehabilitation oversight in functions are at risk if the budget is substantially reduced.

Initiated in 1985, mediation is a relatively new feature of the Michigan workers' compensation system. It serves two primary functions. Mediation is the first line of the dispute resolution system and, over time, has proven to be effective at reducing the number of cases that evolve into full-blown disputes. Mediation is required by statute for some cases,[40] or can be requested by either party. Typically, attorneys are not present, and with the exception of decisions over medical benefits, mediation is nonbinding. Slightly fewer than 40 percent of all statutorily required cases and 70 percent of the voluntarily mediated cases are resolved. During 1991, the average time to a mediation decision was 184.2 days.

The second function performed by the mediators is as an information source for both parties. Mediators advise on statutory requirements and on how to expedite a claim. Research suggests that claimants are often intimidated by the complexity of the workers' compensation claims process, and this information role of mediation is important.[41] The elimination of the mediation function threatens to further clog the formal dispute resolution system by forcing cases to hearing that might have been resolved by mediation. In addition, claimants will turn for information to attorneys who are more likely to push a claim into the formal dispute resolution system.

Consistent with the overall design of the Michigan workers' compensation system, vocational rehabilitation is a privately provided function subject to state oversight. In Michigan, an injured worker is entitled to rehabilitation if the employer is unable to offer employment within that worker's medical restrictions. According to the BWDC, between 2 percent and 5 percent of the people injured on the job could benefit from rehabilitation, although considerably fewer than that receive rehab services.[42] Carriers are required to submit a rehab evaluation report three months after injury and every four months after that. The BWDC reviews all cases extending beyond 120 days for possible rehabilitation needs and follows up to see that these needs are met. Most (90 percent) of the vocational rehabilitation referrals were initiated voluntarily by the carriers, and the number of claimants who returned to work increased steadily over the decade from approximately 600 in 1982 to nearly 3310 in 1991. Throughout the 1980s, the Michigan Rehabilitation system has been viewed as a successful model for other states.

One of the concerns about the effect of the budget cuts of 1992 is that voluntary compliance by carriers will fall, and the BWDC will lack the resources needed for adequate oversight. This is especially a concern in the context of the challenges to the original workers' compensation bargain. Ordinarily, rehabilitation is needed only in the long-term cases with complex injuries. The full scope of rehabilitation can include, among other things, retraining for a new vocation. While this may be highly beneficial to the individual worker and to the larger society, the costs can easily outweigh the benefits for the individual employer. This has always been a problem in workers' compensation, but it will be exacerbated by an increasing number of cases where rehab is needed. The current workers' compensation bargain confines the question of who bears the cost and who receives the benefit of rehabilitation to the individual employment relationship. Unless the injured worker returns to the same employer, under the current arrangement, someone will win and someone will lose.

In the face of a general weakening of the employment relationship, the role of rehabilitation will become increasingly important because returning to the same employer will be a less frequent outcome. The policy question is how to restructure the workers' compensation bargain so that desirable benefits are preserved and costs are fairly distributed.

Because some BWDC functions are jeopardized by funding cuts, some alternative financing schemes have been proposed. One is an employer assessment, such as 1/2 percent of premium. In 1991, $1,259,067,060 of workers' compensation premiums were collected in the Michigan voluntary and assigned risk markets, so such a system would raise over $62 million. This is seen by business as an additional tax and accordingly resisted. This proposal would also fail to generate any revenue from self-insured employers who do not pay premiums, yet account for more than 40 percent of the payroll covered by Michigan workers' compensation law.

A second alternative is to implement user fees. Three have been discussed. One would be an increase in the fee on redemptions, along with a new requirement that attorneys pay part of the increase. This has been criticized as decreasing attorney willingness to represent injured workers. A second suggestion is a self-insurance application fee. Informal estimates suggest that any feasible user fee structure would not raise sufficient revenues to finance the entire system. A third suggestion is that fines be instituted for various participant actions: late filings by carriers, late benefit payments, late insurance terminations, and late policy filings. These proposals have not been costed out to determine whether they would raise sufficient revenues, and, obviously, these estimates need to be made before implementation.

IV. CONCLUSION: WHERE TO GO FROM HERE?

Across the nation, workers' compensation is a troubled program. The current Michigan program has some definite strengths. Open competition has brought costs down from among the highest to below average without generating the coverage availability problems experienced in other states. Michigan's wage-loss system of benefits has allowed the state to avoid an entire class of costly disputes and produces a benefit structure that both parties view as fair for relatively short disabilities. The mediation system is seen by experts in the state as satisfactorily resolving a substantial number of cases and successfully diverting them away from the formal dispute resolution system. And, the state's rehabilitation system is cited nationally as striking a good balance between private provision and public oversight.

While it is clear that the original bargain continues to work well for most claims, there are nevertheless some serious problems facing workers' compensation in Michigan. Many of these can be seen as a manifestation of the conflicting trends of increasing numbers of complex injuries in the context of the weakening employment relationship.

Rising medical costs are an important driver behind the sharp increases in workers' compensation costs to employers and these are partially the result of the shifting composition of injuries, leading to more expensive treatments with more ambiguous results. Increasing backlogs in the dispute resolution system are translating directly into increased costs for all but the self-insured employers. The deterioration of the replacement value of wage-loss benefits for long-term disabilities reveals the inadequacy of the original workers' compensation bargain in dealing with other than simple temporary total cases. The decline in the resources devoted to rehabilitation monitoring threatens the primary existing mechanism in the law to move injured workers back into the labor market once the original employment relationship has been severed.

The policy challenge is to reexamine the original bargain in workers' compensation. This bargain has serious limitations given the current and likely future environment. Part of the challenge will be to accurately assess the strengths of the original bargain and the types of cases it can adequately cover. The larger challenge will be to specify the features of a bargain that will serve the state well into the future.

NOTES

1. The author would like to thank the following experts for sharing their ideas on the critical issues facing workers'compensation in Michigan: Allan Hunt, Tim Hughes, Doug Langham, Michael Madden, Jack Miron, Darryl Tennis, Edward Welch, and Jack Wheatley.
2. Theodore J. St. Antoine, *Workers' Compensation in Michigan: Costs, Benefits, and Fairness*, A Report to Governor James J. Blanchard's Cabinet Council on Jobs and Economic Development, Lansing, Michigan, December 1984.
3. The current workers' compensation program in Michigan has two features that acknowledge that returning to the same job is not always possible and that some injuries sever the work relationship. One is the automatic right to rehabilitation for workers whose employers cannot offer them employment. The second is the presumption that an employee has established a new wage earning capacity after 250 weeks in employments other than the one held at the time of original injury. The first assumes that individual employers are liable for the re-employability of injured workers, while the second limits that liability.

4. St. Antoine, *Workers' Compensation.*
5. Richard Victor, "Major Challenges Facing Workers' Compensation Systems in the 1990's," in *Challenges for the 1990's*, ed., R. A.Victor. (Cambridge, MA: Workers' Compensation Research Institute, 1990).
6. St. Antoine, *Workers' Compensation.*
7. When a case is redeemed or settled, it is likely that the extent of physical impairment is implicit in the settlement, but degree of impairment is not part of the law.
8. Michigan does have a limited set of scheduled benefits. These occur with the loss of specific body parts and are minimum benefits paid regardless of wage loss. The benefits are specified in terms of number of weeks of benefits.
9. Richard M. Skutt, "From Wage Loss to Percentage Disability by Judicial Fiat," *MTLA Quarterly* (Summer 1992): 18-19.
10. The court of appeals has recently agreed to rehear this case after a rehearing was requested by the defendant. No date is set for the rehearing See Welch, "Court of Appeals Redefines Partial Disability," *On Workers' Compensation* 3, no.3 (April 1993): 41.
11. When economic conditions are bad, a wage loss system is thought to be better for workers because they are not forced into an inhospitable labor market due to an injury in the course of work. Impairment systems are better for the employer during bad economic periods because the definition of disability is invariant with labor market conditions. During good economic periods, however, an employer may end up paying benefits to a worker who has experienced impairment but no wage loss.
12. As an aside, this ruling does suggest that the profound challenges facing workers' compensation probably can not be addressed through case law but require statutory action.
13. James N. Ellenberger, "Medical Cost Containment in Workers' Compensation," in *John Burton's Workers' Compensation Monitor*, (Ithaca, NY: LPR Publications, 1990).
14. Fee schedules and utilization review were not the first cost containment measure in Michigan. Michigan also allows the employer to choose the provider for the first ten days of the disability. This contrasts with twenty-five other states that permit unrestricted choice by the employee. See U.S. Chamber of Commerce, Chart IX for a complete list.
15. In one of the interviews held in preparation for this paper, one expert noted that providers have been fairly open about noting that they have shifted their costs away from workers' compensation toward auto cases because they can no longer get the necessary revenues from workers' compensation.
16. Karen Roberts and Susan Zonia, "Income Maintenance Strategies Used by Health Care Providers in Response to Cost Containment Measures in Workers' Compensation," *Journal of Risk and Insurance* (East Lansing: Institute for Public Policy and Social Research, Michigan State University, 1991)
17. It should be noted that it is now over three years since the implementation of the fee schedules and it is possible that the results from this study would not hold for the current period.
18. At least one coalition of providers has formed to protest the fairness of the cost containment rules. Part of the basis of the challenge is that the rules were deter-

mined without sufficient provider input. A counterargument can be made that annual hearings have been held since the implementation of the rules that permit provider testimony about the adequacy of the fee schedule.

19. See Karen Roberts and Sandra Gleason, "Procedural Fairness in the Workers Compensation Claims Process," *The Bulletin of Comparative Labour Relations* (forthcoming). A survey of injured workers by the same researchers found that 12.9 percent of those responding had been denied treatment by providers who did not treat workers' compensation patients. A comparison of those who responded to this survey and the general profile of the workers' compensation claimant population in Michigan suggests that there was no response bias in this survey that would affect this result.

20. The criterion for equitability used in DeVol 1985, was that the after-tax replacement rate was approximately the same across workers with different incomes and number of dependents. The criterion for generosity used in that study was that the replacement rate fell between 80 percent and 100 percent of after-tax lost wages. See Karen DeVol, *Income Replacement for Short Term Disability* (Cambridge MA: Workers' Compensation Research Institute, 1986).

21. There are two exceptions. 1) As a result of the 1980 amendments when workers with dates of injury between 1 September 1965 and 31 December 1979 received a one-time benefit increase based on the inflation rates since the date of injury. See WelchWorkers' *Compensation in Michigan: Law and Practice* (Ann Arbor, MI: Institute of Continuing Legal Education, 1991). 2) ML 418.356 sets forth the conditions under which low-wage individuals with disabilities that exceed two years may receive benefit increases.

22. Karen R. DeVol, *Income Replacement for Long-term Disability: The Role of Workers' Compensation and SSDI,* (Cambridge, MA: Workers Compensation Research Institute, 1986).

23. Currently, ten states use competitive rating; six states have monopoly funds; and the remainder use administered pricing.

24. William Hagar, "The Workers' Compensation Crisis: Can be Dangerous to your Health," presented at the American Risk & Insurance Association Annual Meeting, Washington, D.C., 18 August 1992.

25. See Tillinghast Report, *Responding to the Workers' Compensation Crises (NY: Towers, Perrin,* 1991).

26. See "Spiralling Costs of Workers' Compensation," *Christian Science Monitor* (1 April 1992) and "Fighting the High Costs of Workers' Compensation," *Nation's Business* (March 1990) for examples of anecdotes.

27. Manual rates form the basis for the premiums employers pay for workers' compensation insurance. They are expressed as dollars per hundred dollars of payroll and are supposed to reflect how dangerous a particular occupation (or class code, to use manual rate terminology) is. To determine the actual premium for a specific employer, the manual rates are adjusted by what is called the loss history of that employer. This process, called experience rating, will raise or lower the premium depending on the number and severity of the injuries that occurred in the individual work place. Employers with safer workplaces will pay less for their insurance than employers with more dangerous workplaces.

28. John F. Burton, Jr., H. Allan Hunt, and Alan B. Krueger. *Interstate Variations in the Employers' Costs of Workers' Compensation, with Particular Reference to*

Michigan and the Other Great Lake States, (Ithaca, NY: Workers' Disability Income Systems, Inc., 1985); John F. Burton, Jr. and Timothy P. Schmidle. "The Employers' Costs of Workers' Compensation in Michigan and the Nation," prepared for the Bureau of Workers' Disability Compensation, State of Michigan, November, 1990.

29. Burton and Schmidle, "The Employers' Costs," Table 51.
30. Karen Roberts and Michael Madden. "Equilibrating Tendencies in Workers' Compensation Prices under Open Competition," (Presented at the Annual Meeting of the American Risk and Insurance Association, Washington, D.C., 18 August 1992).
31. St. Antoine, *Workers' Compensation in Michigan,"*
32. *Work Comp Rate Reporter*, (East Lansing, MI: M&R Group, 1992).
33. The mediation program was implemented at the same time. Mediation was expected to reduce the number of cases for which a hearing was requested.
34. Of the 21,191 cases disposed of by the Board of Magistrates in 1991, decisions were made in 1237 cases (5.8 percent); 14,355 (67. percent) cases were redeemed; and 5599 (26.4 percent) were disposed of by miscellaneous awards. See *Michigan Injured Workers*, April-June,1992 for a breakdown of how this varied across magistrates.
35. In the survey of injured workers conducted by Roberts and Gleason, "Procedural Fairness," 55.9 percent of those who contested their claims did not return to the same employer, compared to 15.8 percent of those who did not contest their claim.
36. Class codes are a system of classification that categorizes workers according to risk of injury in the work place.
37. Philip S. Borba and David Appel, "The Propensity of Permanently Disabled Workers to Hire Lawyers," *Industrial and Labor Relations Review* 40, no. 3 (1987): 418-29.
38. Self-insurance is an option in Michigan. Currently 4.39 percent of Michigan employers are self-insured.
39. In addition, a $200 fee is charged on every redemption—$100 paid by the carrier and $100 by the claimant. These fees are deposited into a revolving account that is intended to supplement general appropriations.
40. When a claim is for medical benefits only; when the claim is for a defined period and the employee has returned to work; when the BWDC director requires it.
41. Karen Roberts and Sandra Gleason. "Procedural Fairness in the Workers Compensation Claims Process," *The Bulletin of Comparative Labour Relations*, (forthcoming).
42. State of Michigan, *Annual Report*, Lansing, MI: Bureau of Workers' Disability Compensation, 1990).

III.
Economic Issues
and Urban Policy
in Michigan

The Future of Distressed Communities in Michigan: Rethinking Our Paradigm

Rex L. LaMore

INTRODUCTION

Perhaps more than any other state in the union, Michigan is experiencing a phenomenal transformation. Foreign competition coupled with a rapidly changing manufacturing technology, changing investment patterns, changing social demographics, an aging infrastructure, and a variety of other social and economic factors have forever transformed the state's economy. This transformation is pervasive and unprecedented. It affects the nature of our local economies, the stability of our institutions, the vitality of our communities, and even the structure of our families.

For many of Michigan's citizens and communities, this transformation has offered unprecedented economic prosperity. For others—those who live in isolated rural areas and older inner cities, unskilled or displaced workers, and many women, children, and minorities—this transformation has exacted a heavy toll. Amidst all this change, the "four horsemen" of community decline—*hopelessness, intolerance, ignorance,* and *greed*—flourish in many places in the state, for, in general, it is accurate to observe that Michigan's economic transformation has been unevenly distributed.

Past public policy initiatives to address the needs of distressed communities have, in large part, failed to eliminate the growing levels of persistent poverty and community decline in our state. In this article we will discuss the nature of the problems confronting distressed communities and attempt to identify an alternative paradigm that may serve as a useful guide in the development of effective community and economic development policies and programs appropriate for the unique challenges confronting distressed communities.

STATEMENT OF THE PROBLEM

The United States has one of the highest poverty rates for any western industrialized nation. Almost one in five non-elderly households in the United States were poor in the second half of the 1980s; one in four young households were poor; and over 53 percent of households headed by a lone parent were poor.[1]

In 1979, 10.4 percent of the people in Michigan had incomes at or below the poverty level, while in central cities the figure was 19.5 percent. For the same year, 18.0 percent of the residents of Michigan had incomes at or below 150 percent of the poverty level, and thus can be classified as moderate income.[2] By 1989, the figures had risen to 13.1 percent for poverty level, and 20.5 percent for 150 percent of the poverty level.[3]

Tables 1 through 3 show some of the dynamics involved with identifying low- and moderate-income communities. They also suggest a failure in past public policies to successfully address the problems of distressed communities. In addition they illustrate that low- and moderate-income earners are found in urban areas and in predominately rural counties in Michigan. Obviously, policies aimed at addressing the problems of low- and moderate-income communities must take into account the diversity of people who can be classified as low- and moderate-income.

In almost every instance, poverty levels have increased dramatically between 1979 and 1989. Unemployment trends have been less severe, increasing for some areas and decreasing for others. Obviously, however, such new employment has done little to stem the tide of rising poverty among the residents of the state of Michigan, both urban and rural. The tables also show a disparity of earnings within given geographic boundaries. For instance, during 1989, approximately one-fifth (20.1 percent) of Wayne county's resi-

Table 1.
Poverty and Unemployment Rates for Selected Cities in Michigan
1989

CITY	POVERTY %	UNEMPLOYMENT %
Detroit	32.4	19.7
Flint	30.6	18.3
Battle Creek	18.3	10.3
Grand Rapids	16.1	7.4
Saginaw	31.7	17.9
Jackson	24.7	11.1
Lansing	19.6	8.5
Kalamazoo	26.2	9.2

Source: 1990 U.S. Census, Population Reports

Table 2.
Poverty and Unemployment Rates for Selected Urban Counties in Michigan
1989

COUNTY	POVERTY %	UNEMPLOYMENT %
Wayne	20.1	12.4
Genessee	16.5	10.9
Calhoun	14.3	8.9
Kent	9.2	5.3
Saginaw	17.2	10.5
Jackson	12.0	7.7
Ingham	16.6	6.8
Kalamazoo	13.5	6.2

Source: 1990 U.S. Census, Population Reports

Table 3.
Poverty and Unemployment for Selected Rural
(population < 15,000) Counties in Michigan
1989

COUNTY	POVERTY %	UNEMPLOYMENT %
Alger	14.5	12.2
Baraga	16.8	12.7
Crawford	14.6	9.2
Keweenaw	20.6	17.0
Lake	26.4	17.6
Luce	17.7	10.2
Missaukee	17.3	10.6
Montmorency	17.5	15.5
Oscoda	17.8	10.1
Schoolcraft	16.6	16.6

Source: 1990 U.S. Census, Population Reports

dents were classified as poverty stricken, while the city of Detroit had a poverty rate of 32.4 percent, or nearly one-third. These differences are mirrored in every single listed county/city pair. This *uneven distribution* of income within counties should have policy implications for those charged with addressing the needs of low-income communities in Michigan. Defining the extent of distress in a community offers challenges to practitioners and elected officials. Clearly, measures of income and the levels of unemployment in a community are often used to indicate the level of distress in a given area. Yet, these measures often fail to indicate levels of "underemployment" or of "discouraged workers"—those who have dropped out of the labor force.[4] Other measures include such factors as total tax rate, percent of housing stock built before 1950, percent change in the state equalized value (SEV), change in private sector employment, "jobless rate" (a factor that includes those who are "discouraged"), rate of new business formation, rate of business failures, and change in population.[5]

Each of these measures offers some insight into the health of a local community. It is important to note, however, that static measures of community well-being often fail to recognize severe and sudden events like major plant closing. Additionally, the level of aggregation of these measures may fail to recognize that within communities "pockets of poverty" (poor neighborhoods or poverty levels for women or minorities) may persist in what generally appears to be a relatively healthy local economy.

The fate of Michigan's distressed communities is an integral part of the future of our state. Our willingness to act on the ills confronting our poorest communities will significantly shape the nature of our state well into the next millennium.

Many believe that communities whose economic base has declined are dead or obsolete. Hardly a day goes by without some report of the poor condition of our communities. Poverty, crime, poor infrastructure, inadequate housing, fiscal crisis, civil unrest, and a myriad of other ills confront urban America. It is popular in some circles to suggest that we no longer need our inner cities or smaller rural communities, and that the best solution is to abandon them, let them die. Some are so overwhelmed by the sheer size and complexity of the crisis that they feel a great sense of hopelessness and pessimism for any action. Still others suggest that the future of the United States is in the suburbs or "edge cities," where new office buildings and industrial parks are filling up with thriving businesses that help make us competitive in the global economy.[6] Recent evidence suggests, however, that healthy suburbs are directly linked to prosperous urban cores.[7]

Rural America is also at risk with the demise of inner cities. As people leave unlivable cities, the phenomenon of urban sprawl consumes more and more of our rural landscape. Many prime agricultural lands have already been lost, with many more acres at risk of being developed. Wetlands and wild areas also feel the pressure of human encroachment as people seek healthy livable environments in which to live, work, and play. Unless and until we make our cities livable, there will continue to be pressure on rural lands to make room for more people to live. Yet this phenomenon is both inefficient and detrimental to the nation's long-term sustainable economic prosperity.

Mayor Ray Flynn of Boston, as president of the United States Conference of Mayors in 1991, said:

> No great nation allows its cities to deteriorate. Our competitor nations in the rest of the advanced industrialized world recognize the importance of cities to their economic prosperity. They do not allow their roads, bridges, subways, and other infrastructure to crumble. They do not permit the level of sheer destitution—homelessness, hunger, poverty, and slums—found in America's cities. They invest much more in their urban schools, workers, and families.

It is reasonable to conclude that a healthy, prosperous twenty-first century Michigan must include viable and livable communities.

KEY POLICY QUESTIONS

CAN WE SUCCESSFULLY IDENTIFY THE ROOT CAUSES OF COMMUNITY AND ECONOMIC DISTRESS?

When the United States has successfully identified an issue, we can mobilize and act like no other country in the world. Key to this mobilization is the correct identification and subsequent articulation of a broad based public policy initiative. As we will discuss later in this chapter, we have failed, to date, to adequately identify the root causes of community and economic distress.

Can a long-term comprehensive public policy be developed and implemented to address the root causes of community decline, rather than continuing to promote programs that address only the symptoms of poverty in our communities?

There are no quick fixes to the multifaceted problems of distressed communities. A long-term comprehensive commitment to the revitalization of our communities is essential. No one solution exists, no simple sound-bite analysis coupled with a painless public/private initiative will suffice; no instant gratification will be realized. We must resign ourselves to a long-term comprehensive strategy that will most likely require a great sacrifice on the part of the current generation for the benefit of future generations.

Can a comprehensive interrelated strategy be developed, implemented, and monitored by public institutions?

A comprehensive interrelated strategy is *absolutely essential* because the nature and fabric of our communities are interrelated. For example, the incidence of crime in a community is often related to the availability of employment—higher levels of unemployment generally result in higher incidences of crime; incidences of crime are often related to educational levels—higher levels of crime often are present in communities that have lower levels of formal educational attainment; communities with lower levels of educational achievement often have older housing stocks—older homes often have lower assessed values, which reduce the tax base for school operating funds;[8] communities with low SEVs often have high tax rates, the result of which is a decline or exodus of business, which affects unemployment, which affects crime . . . and on and on and on.

But while the problems of communities are multifaceted and interrelated, clearly requiring a comprehensive strategy to solve them, government is organized into departments, human services are organized into agencies, universities are organized into disciplines. We have very few models or institutional structures in the public sector that can address interrelated issues.

Can a neighborhood-oriented strategy be developed and maintained?

Healthy neighborhoods are the fundamental building blocks of healthy communities. A successful community revitalization strategy must have a neighborhood focus committed to engaging citizens in an empowering process. Neighborhoods experience the community in a holistic way. A community-based focus, committed to a democratic/participatory process has the potential to help address immediate community needs while building their capacity to address future challenges.

Can government develop a flexible program that allows each community to determine its own needs and strategies?

Every community is unique. Therefore, any revitalization strategy must have at its very core a commitment to flexibility to allow each community to develop its own particular strategies. This is essential despite the fact that flexible public initiatives are difficult to evaluate, particularly for "outsiders."

Can those "in power" work to empower the powerless?

There must be a commitment to empowering the residents of our communities. The development of any community revitalization strategy that does not meaningfully engage those living in our communities will not succeed. Solutions imposed from the outside, no matter how well-intentioned, will be met with resistance and fail. Empowered communities give little credence to outside agencies or experts. Once communities are empowered they do not submit easily to the plans and schemes of others. This may represent a threat to the "status quo" of a community. Those "in power" often have reason to fear the empowerment of the powerless.

Can we end social and racial discrimination?

The resolution of the problems of distressed communities will require a commitment to end social and racial discrimination. *This must be a centerpiece of any effective revitalization strategy.* Intolerance—racial, gender, and cultural—must be confronted and treated like the social disease it is.

CURRENT STATE OF AFFAIRS

As our discussion indicates, the problems of low-income and distressed communities offer significant challenges both in understanding the nature of distress as well as suggesting strategies to address these issues.

The problems of low-income and distressed communities have been a major emphasis of government programs since the New Deal era. The 1960s brought the "War on Poverty" and "Great Society" programs, which were specifically targeted to assist minority and low-income communities. While these public policy initiatives represent major federal initiatives in addressing the fate of the poor and disadvantaged in our society, our historic roots in establishing strategies appropriate to the unique challenges of distressed communities are much deeper.

The question of the role of government and public policy in determining the economic well-being of our communities was discussed in the early years of our nation. Thomas Jefferson, a leading proponent of democracy and political self-determination, extended these beliefs to economic matters as well as political. In discussing domestic manufacturing, still a most timely topic as we contemplate international free-trade agreements, Jefferson commented:

> He, therefore, who is now against domestic manufacture, must be for reducing us either to dependence on. . . [foreign nations]. . . or to be clothed in skins, and to live like wild beasts in dens and caverns. . . . Experience has taught me that manufacturers are now as necessary to our independence as to our comfort.[9]

Prior to the late nineteenth century, very few public policy initiatives existed to address the needs of those experiencing hard times. Private charities and religious institutions were the principal organizations attempting to confront the needs of the destitute. Communities whose economic base failed were left to their own demise, as the ghost towns of Michigan's "Copper Country" remind us today.

The work ethic was a strongly held belief, and much of the support for those in hard times emphasized this quality. It wasn't until the 1890s, when the industrial revolution began to displace the need for labor, that there was anything like a general realization that often the "opportunity to work" was not present for many citizens.[10] In fact, the depression of the 1890s is a particularly appropriate historical event in considering our present situation. This depression was precipitated by the advent of the industrial age. Technological advancements had produced severe hardships and disrupted the nature of work as it was normally understood at the time.

Yet efforts to help those in need have almost always attempted to reinforce the strongly held belief in the work ethic and avoid direct handouts. This belief remains today, as evidenced by the newly implemented state of Michigan "Social Contract" program, which requires that individuals receiving assistance from the state who are not currently enrolled in an educational or job training program must "volunteer"(i.e., work for nothing) to qualify for assistance.

Recent economic development and human service responses to the needs of distressed communities have sought to encourage greater self-help and entrepreneurial strategies. According to economic "trickle-down," a widely held economic development policy, the idea was that generating greater wealth for the wealthy, i.e., creating a larger economic pie, would benefit the poor. The fallacy of these strategies are now widely apparent. The deregulation of the banking industry has brought about the biggest scandal in the financing industry in recent history; the abandonment of a public housing policy has resulted in a crisis in housing; the promises of enterprise zones and industrial development policies have produced few gains for state and local governments; and poverty soared in the 1980s.[11]

Strategies to create jobs and provide needed goods and services in distressed communities are critical to the revitalization of the state's economy. To some extent we have failed to accurately understand the nature of poverty in communities and, therefore, we have not produced effective public policy initiatives to address the unique challenges of these communities.

RETHINKING THE BASIC PROBLEM

The problem of poor communities is much more substantive than just the lack of economic resources as measured through indicators of income and employment. Clearly these communities have limited resources and wealth, but these are merely symptoms of a deeper problem. The root of their poverty is in the lack of control residents have in providing for their own needs. In his book *Communities on the Way*, Stewart Perry noted this phenomenon in the early 1960s. He describes how impoverished communities were not helped by past economic and community development strategies because these efforts ignored "the cultural tools by which the community lives." He points out that "the ideas, attitudes, preferences, and values embodied in the local perspective are expressed in the institutions of the community that produce the decisions on development—that is, decisions on changes that are crucial to reversing the impoverishment of the community."[12]

S. Perry[13] defines community economic development as:

> . . . the creation or strengthening of economic organiza-
> tions (or more technically, economic institutions) that are
> controlled or owned by the residents of the area in which
> they are located or in which they will exert primary influ-
> ence. The institutions that are owned or controlled locally
> can include such forms as business firms, industrial devel-
> opment parks, housing development corporations, banks,
> credit unions, cooperatives, and community development
> corporations. . . . They might also include organizations
> (or services) that upgrade the human and social environ-
> ment in such a way as to increase the economic value and
> energy of the community.

As L.M. Gardner[14] pointed out:

> The basic problem of poverty communities is that they
> are poor. Poor not only because little money enters the
> community, but also because the money coming in flows
> out very quickly, leaving the community few resources. .
> . . The lack of institutions based in and responsive to poor
> communities causes a systematic drain of money from
> them.

We can conclude from this discussion that the problem of distressed communities is not only that they have limited resources, but
that they do not have local institutions that are responsive to or controlled by the community. This suggests a different strategy for the
revitalization of these communities than has been pursued through
traditional development strategies. This paradigm suggests that the
successful revitalization of distressed communities will require a commitment to the building of local institutions controlled by and
responsive to the needs of low-income residents, an *institutional*
development strategy or, as defined by Perry, community economic
development.

Michigan has relatively limited experience in building the institutional capacity of distressed communities. Efforts like the
Neighborhood Builders Alliance and the Neighborhood Assistance
and Participation Program had a number of limitations, including
limited financial support, poorly defined goals, and limited targeting

to distressed areas.[15] Similarly, local governments have had limited success in developing and sustaining long-term comprehensive institutional development strategies targeted to distress areas.

Recent efforts like the Wayne County Urban Recovery Partnership are encouraging signs in the development of public initiatives that both recognize the comprehensive and long-term nature of the problems confronting our most distressed areas.

In an analysis of state programs designed to facilitate community economic development[16] several characteristics seemed to be significant. These include:

- The provision of technical assistance to organizations
- Basic core support (funding for staff and daily operations) for organizations and organizational development efforts
- Financial support for pre-development activities
- Grants or equity to organizations for investment in development activities
- Debt financing of development activities

The provision of support for "emerging groups" (groups with limited track records in community and economic development) is a critical element of a successful community-based institutional development strategy. Providing financial support for "deals" will have a limited impact, particularly in those communities that are the most distressed and often least organized. Unfortunately, very few state or local governments are currently prepared to commit to this type of developmental strategy.

One final element appears to be particularly important in examining the role of government in facilitating community-based institutional development—that is the role of local governments. Local governments have traditionally played significant roles in fostering or inhibiting community-based organizations in distressed communities. Historically, local governments have maintained the dominant role in officially sanctioning the efforts of local institutions to undertake revitalization efforts. In many cases, community-based initiatives have sought to change the *status quo* in a community, even against the wishes of the elected and appointed officials of local governments. A public policy that seeks to empower community-based initiatives may find strong opposition from local governments.

CONCLUSION

It is important to stress the immense barriers that distressed communities face in their efforts to create jobs and provide needed goods and services. It is unlikely, given the complexity and interrelatedness of these issues, that any single public policy initiative, no matter how well conceived or funded, will ultimately overcome the significant financial and social barriers these communities face. These seemingly overwhelming barriers have convinced some critics that nothing can be done to stimulate revitalization. The experience and track record of community economic development initiatives, however, runs contrary to this conclusion. A long-term comprehensive commitment to empowering communities has the demonstrated potential to change the downward spiral of decline in these communities. The challenge confronting policymakers today is to implement the new institutional structures based on this changing paradigm.

NOTES

1. Joint Center for Political and Economic Studies (1991). "Poverty, Inequality and Crisis of Social Policy," summary findings, (Washington, D.C.: Joint Center for Political and Economic Studies, 1991), 1.
2. U.S. Census, *Population Reports, 1980.* (Washington, D.C.: Government Printing Office).
3. U.S. Census, *Population Reports, 1990,* (Washington, D.C.: Government Printing Office); Also, Conversation with State of Michigan Demographer's Office.
4. Northeast-Midwest Institute, "Measure of Economic Distress." (Washington, D.C.: Northeast-Midwest Institute 1977), 1-4.
5. Michigan Department of Commerce, "Michigan Small Cities Program. Need Index Ranking," (Lansing, Mich.: Michigan Department of Commerce,1985)
6. J. Persky, E. Schar, and W. Wreich, "Does Americans Need Cities." (Washington, D.C.: Economic Policy Institute, 1991), 2.
7. H. Savitch, "Detroit's Ill Health Hurts Suburbs Too." *Detroit Free Press,* 9 January 1992, 91.
8. Michigan League for Human Services, "K-12 Pubic Education in Michigan." (Lansing, Mich.: Michigan League for Human Services, 1992), 24.
9. John Sharp Williams, (1913) "Thomas Jefferson: His Permanent Influence on American Institutions." (New York: Columbia University Press, 1913), 152.
10. R. H. Grant, *Self-help in the 1890's. Depression.* (Ames: Iowa State University Press, 1983).
11. P. Nyden and W. Wiewel, *Challenging Uneven Development: An Urban Agenda for the 1990's,* (New Brunswick, N.J.: Rutgers University Press, 1990), x.
12. Stawart Perry, *Communities on the Way,* Albany: State University of New York Press, 1987), 36-37.

13. S. Perry, *Federal Support for CDC's. Some History and Issues of Community Control.*(Cambridge, Mass.: Center for Community Change, 1973), 16.

14. L. M. Gardner, "Creating Successful Businesses." *Community Economic Development Strategies*, vol. 1. (Berkeley, Calif.: National Economic Development and Law Center, 1983), 4.

15. Center for Urban Affairs, "The Michigan Neighborhood Builders Alliance Program: An Evaluation." East Lansing, Mich.: Center for Urban Affairs, Michigan State University, 1992.

16. R. LaMore, "Recent Directions and Perspective on Community Economic Development." In *Contemporary Urban America,* ed. Marvel Lang (New York: University Press of America,1991), 310.

The State of Black Michigan

Joe T. Darden

THE PROBLEM

In the late 1960s, a report prepared by the Kerner Commission (appointed by the President) concluded that America was moving toward two societies—one black and one white, separate and unequal.[1] Michigan, with its 1.3 million blacks constituting 14 percent of the state's population, can be considered a microcosm of the nation as a whole. Michigan, too, has been moving toward two separate and unequal societies.

A discussion of Michigan's pattern of racial separation—its extent, consequences, and what policies are necessary to reverse the trend—constitutes the basic focus of this chapter.

The problem of increasing racial inequality is important for all Michigan citizens. What is at stake is a future of continuing apartheid with the probability of increased racial conflict or a future moving strongly toward equality and the prospect of racial harmony.

The thesis of this chapter is that the increasing inequality between blacks and whites is rooted in persistent racial discrimination, uneven economic investment, and structural changes in the state's economy. As long as these practices exist, there is a strong probability that the situation will worsen, as population mobility within the state continues to reinforce patterns of economic, social, and racial inequality, contributing to more racial and class conflict.

Previous and present policies related to employment, housing, and education have been insufficient, since blacks in Michigan continue to face an interrelated web of racial discrimination in housing, education, and employment. Racial inequality is constantly reinforced by racial discrimination, which limits black social, economic, and spatial mobility.

Discrimination is a primary contributor to housing segregation, which limits blacks' access to high-quality, desegregated educational opportunities. Housing segregation also limits their information about and access to suburban jobs, which hold promise of stability, decent pay, and advancement potential.

Segregated schools in poor central city districts provide fewer opportunities for achievement and the attainment of equal educational credentials for black students than for their white suburban counterparts. In other words, most blacks in Michigan are isolated in economic areas of no growth in central cities, while the economic opportunities are expanding in predominantly white suburban areas. Furthermore, employers are more likely to hire job seekers whose physical and cultural attributes, i.e. race and background, are similar to their own and/or their present employees. Employers are also more likely to hire employees who attended schools and live in neighborhoods similar to those of their present employees. These constrained opportunities make it more probable that blacks will be the least likely group to be hired.[2]

Thus, discrimination and segregation in housing, schools, and employment systematically create and perpetuate social and economic inequality between blacks and whites. Such inequality is intensified by uneven economic investment and structural changes in the state's economy.

2. THE CURRENT STATE OF AFFAIRS

Most of the material presented in this chapter was derived from the research findings in the 1984-1992 issues of *The State of Black Michigan*—a series of annual reports published by Urban Affairs Programs at Michigan State University in cooperation with the Michigan Council of Urban League Executives.

Since 1984, thirty-five authors from Michigan State University, The University of Michigan, Oakland University, and Wayne State University have contributed forty-six chapters dealing with current problems involving the status of Michigan's black citizens. When possible, comparisons have been made between the status of Michigan's black citizens and that of Michigan's white citizens.[3]

The research findings presented in the nine issues of *The State of Black Michigan* have consistently confirmed the existence of a widening socioeconomic gap between Michigan's blacks and whites. A discussion of the extent and nature of that inequality is presented in the following sections.

UNEMPLOYMENT

In 1985, *The State of Black Michigan* report revealed that black unemployment rates in Michigan had been in the double digits in all years since 1970, averaging 18.1 percent through 1982 and had been two to three times the rates for whites.[4]

At the time, blacks were told by some state policymakers to be patient and trust in the general recovery, and that the persistent gaps would be removed. Blacks were told that Michigan was in the midst of a strong economic recovery and that a rising tide would lift all boats.[5]

One of the authors of *The State of Black Michigan's 1985* report (Karl Gregory) examined the extent to which the recovery benefited blacks and reduced the racial gap. Gregory found that, historically, each recession in Michigan has ended with the black unemployment rate higher than at the end of the previous recession, suggesting a cumulative worsening of the unemployment experience by blacks, and/or an increased ineffectiveness of public and private economic policies. At the end of the recession in the early 1970s, the non-white unemployment rate reached a calendar-year high in Michigan of 14.9 percent in 1972; it rose to 21 percent in 1975, the year of the trough of that recession; and to 33.4 percent in 1982.[6] According to Gregory, even in the Great Depression (1932), the top overall unemployment rate in the United States reached only 25 percent.

When Detroit and other Michigan cities exploded in 1967 in one of the worst black rebellions in Michigan's history, the non-white unemployment rate was 11 percent, compared with a white rate of 3.3 percent. The non-white/white ratio was more than three times the rate for whites.[7]

Four years after Detroit and other Michigan cities experienced massive violence, the black unemployment rate in the state had risen to 14 percent, compared with a white rate of 6.9 percent. Between 1971 and 1982, the black unemployment rate steadily increased, reaching its peak of 33.4 percent in 1982. The white rate, on the other hand, rose to 13.3 percent in 1982.

The American automobile industry has been a major provider of employment for black workers. Any major decline in black employment in the automobile industry had to have a severe negative impact on black Michigan's socioeconomic well-being and opportunities for socioeconomic mobility. Due to the traditional concentration of black jobs in this industry and the heavy reliance on those jobs for their collective contribution to economic well-being, the consequences of a major decline in the employment sector was far-reaching for blacks.[8]

The job losses in the auto industry were not evenly distributed—the greatest being in the metropolitan areas where the black population is most heavily concentrated. Since blacks have been so dependent on automobile manufacturing jobs, their economic well-being is disproportionately deteriorating as a consequence. Unlike most white workers, most black workers have had no apparent alternative source of new jobs offering decent wages and benefits to offset this economic loss.[9] In sum, the declines in the absolute levels of employment in both the automobile and manufacturing industries raised the unemployment rates for black males, white males, black females, and white females. However, the effect of such declines has been disproportionately larger for blacks, so that the black-white unemployment gap has been widened by the declines.

Further, the declining shares of employment in the automobile sector are estimated to have exerted relatively high differential effects on black-white unemployment patterns, apparently because industrial shifts have been accompanied by the relative success of whites to obtain replacement jobs in the alternative nonindustrial sector.[10] Indeed, Fosu found that the declining share of industrial employment had little or no negative impact on white female unemployment. Meanwhile, its effect on black male unemployment was roughly 4 times that for white males.[11]

Such persistently wide gaps in unemployment rates and the disproportionate impact by race can have implications for racial conflict and partisan politics.

Unemployment rates have traditionally had a strong impact on partisan politics. Many voters endorse one candidate or the other with the hope that their individual situation will improve through a reduction in the unemployment rate.

Most blacks in Michigan have traditionally voted Democratic in elections for governor with the hope that a Democratic administration would assist in reducing the high rate of black unemployment. However, an examination of the impact of a Democratic administration on black unemployment in Michigan revealed a disappointing outcome.

Black rates of unemployment were higher, and the unemployment gap between blacks and whites wider under the Democratic administration of Governor Blanchard (1983 to 1988) than under the Republican administration of Governor Milliken (1971 to 1982). For both males and females, the black unemployment rate was roughly 2.25 times the white rate during the 1971-1982 Republican regime, and about 3 times the white rate during the subsequent Democratic administration (1983-1988). For youths, black unemployment was greater by 2.5 times in the Republican regime and by 3.25 times in the Democratic regime.[12]

Trends in unemployment rates showed an increase for both blacks and whites during the Republican administration, while the trends showed a decrease under the Democratic administration that followed. However, the rates of unemployment were never lowered to the level of the rates under the Republican administration.

The black-white unemployment gap remained relatively constant during the Republican governorship, but the gap appears to have widened under the Democratic administration. Fosu argues that the reason for this phenomenon is that the unemployment rate fell proportionately more for whites than for blacks under Governor Blanchard's administration during the period 1983-1988.[13]

HOUSING

Like employment, accessibility to housing has also been unequal for blacks in Michigan. Despite passage of the Federal Fair Housing Act of 1968, and Michigan's Elliott-Larson Civil Rights Act of 1977, most blacks in Michigan have continued to live in racially segregated housing. In 1990, the mean level of segregation in the twelve metropolitan areas in the state was 68.8 percent, based on an index of dissimilarity,[14] reflecting an increase in segregation in six of the twelve metropolitan areas between 1980 and 1990.

The Detroit metropolitan area, where most blacks in Michigan live, remained (in 1990) the most racially segregated metropolitan area in the state and the nation with an index of 87.4 percent (virtually the same level that existed in 1960—i.e., before passage of the Federal Fair Housing Act and Michigan's Elliott-Larson Civil Rights Act).

Apparently, these two pieces of legislation have had virtually no impact on reducing the high level of residential segregation in Metropolitan Detroit.[15]

Although blacks have increasingly moved to the suburbs of metropolitan areas after passage of the Federal Fair Housing Act in 1968, black suburbanization has not been synonymous with black residential desegregation. Blacks in the suburbs were more residentially segregated from whites in 1990 than were blacks who remained in central cities. Furthermore, the proportion of the black population (compared with that of whites) living in the suburbs has remained small.

Only suburban Detroit, Ann Arbor, Benton Harbor, Flint, and Muskegon had more than 10,000 blacks in 1990. Most were concentrated in satellite cities rather than in traditional suburban municipalities.[16]

Inasmuch as blacks in Michigan are disproportionately located in central cities, a higher percentage (compared with that for whites) are more likely to live in older, overcrowded housing.[17]

It appears that the housing market in Metropolitan Detroit, and other metropolitan areas in Michigan, have not been allowed to operate without intervention. Race-conscious intervention to segregate the races by means of racial steering and other forms of racial discrimination in housing has been pervasive. This intervention denies equal access to housing, in violation of the 1968 U.S. Fair Housing Law and Michigan's 1977 Elliott-Larson Civil Rights Act. As a result, considering a black and a white of equal socioeconomic status, it is a high probability that the white will reside in a better neighborhood with better schools, municipal services, and other quality-of-life factors.

Discrimination results in lower-, middle-, and upper-class blacks living in closer proximity on the average than do lower-, middle-, and upper-class whites. Such clustering of blacks, regardless of class, is often mistakenly attributed (by most whites) to black preference for segregated living. Most whites have a tendency to comfort themselves with the belief that most blacks want to live in black neighborhoods. It is true, after all, that most whites prefer to live in white neighborhoods.[18] What is often overlooked is the factor of differential quality of the neighborhoods by race, resulting in differential motivation by blacks (compared with whites) for integrated neighborhoods. Whereas white neighborhood location can be assessed in terms of preference, black neighborhood location must be assessed in terms of constraints that have prevented the fulfillment of preferences.[19] Thus, it is not black preference for segregation but racial discrimination in housing that is the major factor in black residential segregation.[20]

A 1991-released National Housing Discrimination Study, which included metropolitan Detroit among its twenty-five metro areas, revealed that black home-seekers were experiencing some form of discrimination in at least half of their encounters with sales and rental agents. The estimated overall incidence of discrimination was 56 percent for black renters, and 59 percent for black home seekers.[21]

Discrimination in housing remains a major factor behind the high level of residential segregation in Metropolitan Detroit. Housing segregation also impacts accessibility to quality education.

EDUCATION

The Original Formulation of the Problem

In 1954, when the U.S. Supreme Court became involved in shaping the nation's civil rights policy in the area of public education, the problem could be defined as "the denial, due to race, of equal access to quality education within school districts." There were racially separate *intra district* public schools established and maintained by state laws in the "Deep South." Such schools were also unequal in the quantity and quality of resources and in the quality of education received by students attending "white schools" compared with that received by students attending "black schools."

In Michigan and other states outside the "Deep South," black students were also often denied equal access to a quality education. This inequality did not necessarily result from the establishment and maintenance of racially separate schools through state law, but rather resulted from various covert acts of local school boards, in Detroit, Kalamazoo, and other central cities in the state. Whether in the South or elsewhere, the outcome was similar: the maintenance of racially separate and unequal *intra district* public schools.

Past Policies to Desegregate Schools

To address the problem, the U.S. Supreme Court ruled in 1954 that state-sanctioned segregation is "inherently unequal" and "has no place in the field of public education."[22]

Driven by a desire to maintain white supremacy, a position whites had enjoyed for so long, there were numerous attempts by state and local governmental authorities in Michigan and other areas to nullify the new policy of desegregation through covert measures to circumvent its application, and through a variety of strategies designed to delay or minimize its ultimate impact.[23]

Although a majority of Michigan's policymakers may have accepted school desegregation as a worthwhile goal, their predominantly white constituents did not. Some whites may have accepted desegregation in principle, but most opposed it in practice. Thus, continued enforcement generated political pressure to curb desegregation policy in Michigan and elsewhere by curbing the policymaking powers of specific branches of government.[24]

Due to continued opposition by most whites to the enforcement of school desegregation policy, criticism of the role of the courts in public policymaking increased. The legitimacy and capacity of the courts in mandating sweeping institutional reforms were questioned.[25] Some observers have argued that it was because of the very effectiveness of certain federal policies that the role of the federal courts was coming under attack.[26]

Increased opposition to school desegregation in Michigan culminated in the 1974 Supreme Court decision that rejected metropolitan desegregation in Detroit. The metropolitan desegregation plan, if left intact, would have desegregated predominantly black Detroit and fifty-two surrounding predominantly white suburban school districts.[27]

The impact of the *Milliken* decision on urban school desegregation was a severe setback not only in Michigan, but in large urban school districts throughout the country.[28]

In Michigan, following the *Milliken* decision, the distribution of black students revealed a pattern of persistent racial concentration. In 1976-77, over 96 percent of all black students in Michigan public schools were enrolled in only forty school districts (out of a total of 530). Thirteen years later, in 1989-90, approximately 94 percent of all black students in Michigan were enrolled in the same forty school districts (out of a total of 525).[29]

During the 1989-90 school year, 78 percent of all black public school students in Michigan, compared with 78.9 percent in 1976-77, were attending schools with more than 50 percent non-white enrollment. Only 22 percent of black students attended schools that were predominantly white in 1989-90. This was about the same as the 21.1 percent of black students attending predominantly white schools in 1976.[30]

Of greater importance is the fact that the districts where most black students attend school are located in central cities. They are usually poorer, and depend on the state of Michigan for 50 percent or more of their operating revenue. These districts also tend to have higher tax rates and declining tax bases.[31]

The persistent fiscal disparities between predominantly black and predominantly white school districts in Michigan have some influence on instructional impact and consequently on pupil performance outcomes. Students in poorer central city school districts in Michigan have lower average achievement scores than students in more affluent suburban school districts. Although other factors also contribute to student outcomes, abundant fiscal resources to pay teachers and purchase equipment and technology clearly provide educational options or enhancements that cannot be provided in dependent impoverished school districts.[32]

A lack of commitment to equal access to quality education through desegregation continues in Michigan. With the persistent gap in black and white achievement and the high number of one-race schools, it is apparent that the objective of *Brown* (i.e., providing equal access to a quality education for all students) has not been accomplished. The changes needed to achieve that goal can be seen by reformulating the desegregation problem.

A Reformulation of the Problem

Despite the *Milliken* decision in 1974, the most important change now necessary to begin steps toward achieving equal access to quality education through desegregation is to shift remedial policies from an *intra district* to an *inter district* focus.

Unlike thirty years ago, when school desegregation could be achieved *within* a city school district, today the pattern of demographics, involving the shift of most white children to the suburbs and the increasing concentration of most black and Hispanic children in the city,[33] makes meaningful desegregation *within* central city school districts difficult.

Furthermore, the property tax system in Michigan perpetuates inequities in school financing. Since predominantly black districts are also disproportionately poorer, the resources to maintain a high-quality education system will continue to be less than those in richer, predominantly white suburban districts. As long as the property tax serves as the basis for school financing, *intra district* school desegregation as a process to achieve equal access to a quality education will be problematic.

Policies to Address the Problem

Viable policies to address the problem of inequality must include a combination of incentives and disincentives.

1. Unemployment

- Black unemployment can be most effectively addressed through bold policies in job creation and retraining, involving both the public and private sectors.
- In the short term, a job creation policy focusing on government (i.e., public sector) investment to rebuild the urban infrastructure in Michigan, combined with job retraining of displaced manufacturing workers and others for new types of jobs, seems the most promising approach. The urban physical infrastructure, broadly defined, includes roads and bridges, housing stock, schools, other public buildings, parks, recreational facilities, public transit, and waste disposal systems.[34] An investment in rebuilding these structures is "an investment in rebuilding Michigan," while creating more jobs and reducing the high black unemployment rate. Such investment, at the same time, can offer opportunities for black urban residents to obtain apprentice-type skills training in a variety of job categories.[35]

  Furthermore, initiatives to rebuild urban communities in Michigan by upgrading the infrastructure will motivate business and industry to engage in private investment, and expand and improve tourism opportunities.
- Such long-term investment initiatives should be led by the private sector with the State of Michigan and local governments providing a variety of tax incentives to revitalize urban communities. These tax incentives may include but should not necessarily be limited to, enterprise zones.

Caution is advised, however, on any policy dealing with enterprise zones. First, to be successful, the tax incentives must be of sufficient magnitude to attract substantial private investment, thereby creating an adequate number of jobs; and second, the enterprise zone legislation must be targeted to restrict employment to the unemployed workers actually residing in the depressed zone. This requirement can help to reduce the high rate of unemployment of the residents in the area and can stimulate economic development of the area itself.[36]

Without such targeting, enterprise zones are unlikely to succeed in reducing the high rate of black unemployment and narrowing the black-white unemployment gap in Michigan.

2. Unequal Access to Housing: Background and Rationale

Most empirical evidence points to discrimination, not income or preferences, as the major barrier to fair housing.[37] Economic factors are of minor importance. Since blacks are not an ethnic group in the way in which foreign-born families once were, voluntary segregation is unlikely except as a response to intimidation. Thus, black segregation is largely compelled.[38] As a result, it remains severe, widespread, unresponsive to black economic improvement, and impervious to the assimilative processes that dispersed ethnic groups.

Recent research suggests that the most effective way to remove barriers to fair housing is through a combination of economic incentives and economic disincentives. There should be economic incentives for those who take action to remove the barriers and economic disincentives through penalties for those who act to maintain barriers.[39]

The removal of the barriers to fair housing will result in an expansion of the housing options for blacks and other racial minorities throughout cities and suburbs so that the housing options of racial minorities equal the options of the white majority. To achieve this goal requires bold, creative leadership on the part of the federal government, state government, local government, public school systems, and the private sector.

Such a plan must go beyond affirmative marketing to include "integration incentives." Affirmative marketing is an effort to promote integration or prevent segregation by taking special steps to provide information about available housing to persons or racial groups who, without such efforts, would not be likely to know of the availability of, or to express an interest in, the homes or apartments being offered. An "integration incentive" plan not only promotes integration by providing information about available housing to both whites and non-whites where they are underrepresented, but provides an incentive that makes it economically advantageous to purchase or rent such housing.

The policy recommendations that follow are divided into two parts: 1) incentives to desegregate; and 2) disincentives to discriminate.

3. Unequal Access to Quality Education

A viable education policy at the state level must provide economic incentives for the following:

- Urban school bureaucracy must be restructured and directed toward greater decision-making, empowerment, and participation of teachers and parents in aspects such as curriculum development and hiring of administrative personnel.

- Districts must be assisted in relating teacher salaries to merit (as determined by progress in student achievement).
- Districts need to be assisted in relying less on the property tax to fund public schools.
- Districts must be encouraged to participate in "metropolitan-wide open enrollment" programs that would allow students in urban as well as suburban public schools to attend any public school of their choice in the metropolitan area, with transportation provided by the state with some assistance from the federal government where needed.
- Economic support must be provided for Head Start (pre-kindergarten) programs in every poor urban school.
- Economic rewards must be provided to districts that effectively diversify the racial composition of the work force (i.e., teachers and administrators).

Incentives to Desegregate

- The State of Michigan should provide substantial tax deductions to any family that purchases a home in an area where members of its racial group are underrepresented.
- The state and local governments should provide low (i.e., below-market-rate) interest loans to any family that purchases a home in an area where members of its racial group are underrepresented.
- The state and local governments should provide loans at even lower interest rates to families who send their children to public schools where their own race is underrepresented, since the quality and racial composition of the public schools are important factors influencing young families' choice of neighborhoods.
- The state and local governments should provide tax deductions to real estate firms according to the proportion of sales made to families in areas of racial underrepresentation.

In order for such an "integration incentive" plan to work, it must be metropolitan in scope and must involve effective partnerships between representatives of the federal government, state government, local government, real estate and banking industry, and fair housing centers or other community or neighborhood-based organizations. Such partnerships, however, will not be sufficient as long as there is racial steering and/or racial discrimination.

Disincentives to Discriminate

A vigorous attack on racial steering and/or discrimination must occur if the integration incentive plan is to work. A successful attack on racial steering and discrimination will require the use of the most effective tools to date: 1) testing, and 2) lawsuits resulting in substantial economic penalties in order to serve as economic disincentives.

Following are specific recommendations with respect to disincentives to discriminate and/or steer to segregate.

- Concerned citizens of Michigan should establish fair housing centers in sufficient numbers and in strategic areas in order to monitor discrimination problems in housing and to provide effective remedies.
- The state and local governments should provide sufficient financial support to fair housing centers so that they may be able to employ full-time professional testers or inspectors to detect violators in the housing industry.
- Fair housing centers, in cooperation with attorneys and plaintiffs (i.e., victims of discrimination), should file a sufficient number of lawsuits, using the data gathered through testing, so that the suits will serve as a deterrent against acts of unlawful discrimination.
- The State of Michigan's Department of Licensing and Regulation should vigorously enforce regulations that would lead to revoking licenses of real estate brokers found guilty of discrimination.

To date, testing remains the most effective tool to assess the extent of discrimination in housing. The processing of complaints alone will never solve the discrimination problem, since it is likely that complaints far underrepresent the actual extent of discrimination.

Testing must be expanded to become a full-time occupation in which individuals are trained and employed to detect discrimination. Just as the city, state, and federal governments employ inspectors to detect unlawful acts in other areas of life, the government must employ testers or inspectors to detect violators in the housing industry.

In the final analysis, if the Fair Housing Act is to be a deterrent, it must convince a potential violator that illegal acts will be detected and punished with a high degree of certainty.[40]

The use of both "incentives to desegregate" and "disincentives to discriminate," with a strong attack on racial steering and racial discrimination, may provide the best approach for Michigan metropolitan areas to substantially reduce their persistent patterns of racial residential segregation.

SUMMARY

It has been demonstrated that the state of black Michigan is suffering from the effects of double digit unemployment (with rates for blacks at least twice those for whites), unequal education, and housing segregation.

The evidence seems to suggest that these effects are related to an interlocking web of relationships involving discrimination—direct or indirect—based on race. Such discrimination leads to persistent inequality—which is intensified by uneven investment and structural changes in the state's economy.

Apparently, past and/or present policies have not been sufficient to address the problem. This chapter has offered a set of policy options involving economic incentives and disincentives in each area—employment, education, and housing.

Policy formulation and implementation will require bold leadership on the part of policymakers. In the absence of such policies, Michigan's blacks and whites will continue to move toward two separate and unequal societies with the potential for increased racial conflict.

NOTES

1. National Advisory Commission on Civil Disorders. *A Report to the Commission.* New York: E.P. Dutton and Co., 1968).
2. Joe T. Darden, H. Duleep, and G. Galster, "Civil Rights in Metropolitan America." *Journal of Urban Affairs* 14 (September 1992): 469-96.
3. Frances Thomas, ed. *The State of Black Michigan.* (East Lansing: Urban Affairs Programs, Michigan State University, 1991; 1992).
4. Karl Gregory, "Toward a Strategy for Economic Development in the Black Community." In *The State of Black Michigan, 1985*, ed. Frances Thomas, 47-63. (East Lansing: Urban Affairs Programs, Michigan State University, 1985).
5. Ibid.
6. Ibid.
7. Karl Gregory, "Trends in the Economic Status of Michigan Blacks Since 1967." In *The State of Black Michigan, 1987*, ed. Frances Thomas, 3-18. (East Lansing: Urban Affairs Programs, Michigan State University, 1987).
8. Donald R. Deskins, "Michigan's Restructured Automotive Industry: Its Impact on Black Employment." In *The State of Black Michigan, 1988*, ed. Frances Thomas, 9-18. (East Lansing: Urban Affairs Programs, Michigan State University, 1988).
9. Ibid.

10. Augustin Fosu, "Industrial Change and Black-White Unemployment Patterns in Michigan, 1971-1990." In *The State of Black Michigan, 1992,* ed. Frances Thomas, 3-12. (East Lansing: Urban Affairs Programs, Michigan State University, 1992).

11. Ibid.

12. Augustin Fosu, "Black Unemployment in Michigan Under Democratic and Republican Governors." In *The State of Black Michigan, 1990,* ed. Frances Thomas, 3-7. (East Lansing: Urban Affairs Programs, Michigan State University, 1990).

13. Ibid.

14. The index of dissimilarity ranges from "0" indicating no segregation to "100" indicating complete segregation. The higher the index, the greater is the degree of segregation, For a detailed discussion of the computation of the index, see Joe T. Darden and Arthur Tabachneck, "Algorithm 8: Graphic and Mathematical Descriptions of Inequality, Dissimilarity, Segregation, and Concentration," *Environment and Planning A,* 12 (1980): 227-34.

15. Joe T. Darden, (1992). "Residential Segregation of Blacks in Metropolitan Areas of Michigan, 1960-1990." In *The State of Black Michigan, 1992,* ed. Frances Thomas, (East Lansing: Urban Affairs Programs, Michigan State University, 1992).

16. Ibid.

17. Joe T. Darden, "The Housing Situation of Blacks in Metropolitan Areas of Michigan." In *The State of Black Michigan, 1985,* ed. Frances Thomas, 11-21. (East Lansing: Urban Affairs Programs, Michigan State University, 1985).

18. Joe T. Darden, "Choosing Neighbors and Neighborhoods: The Role of Race in Housing using Preference." In *Divided Neighborhoods: Changing Patterns of Racial Segregation,* ed. Gary A. Tobin, 15-42, vol. 32, *Urban Affairs Annual Reviews.* (Beverly Hills: Sage Publications, 1987).

19. William H. Frey, "Lifecourse Migration of Metropolitan Whites and Blacks and the Structure of Demographic Change in Large Central Cities." *American Sociological Review* 49 (1984): 803-27.

20. Darden, "Choosing Neighbors and Neighborhoods".

21. M. Turner, R.J. Struyk, and J. Yinger, *Housing Discrimination Study: Synthesis.* (Washington, D.C.: U.S. Department of housing and Urban Development, Office of Policy Development and Research, 1991).

22. *Brown v. Board of Education,* 347 U.S. 483, 1954.

23. Charles Vergon, "School Desegregation: Lessons from Three Decades of Experience." *Education and Urban Society* 23 (1990): 22-49; Joe T. Darden, R. Hill, J. Thomas, and R. Thomas, *Detroit: Race and Uneven Development.* (Philadelphia: Temple University Press, 1987).

24. Vergon, "School Desegregation."

25. Nathan Glazer, "Towards an Imperial Judiciary?" *The Public Interest* 41 (1975): 104-23; D. Horowitz, *The Courts and Social Policy.* (Washington, D.C.: The Brookings Institution, 1977).

26. C. Kastle and M. Smith, "The Federal Role in Elementary and Secondary Education, 1949-1980." *Harvard Education Review* 34, no. 4 (1980): 564-83.

27. *Milliken v. Bradley,* U.S. 418, 1974.

28. Percy Bates, "The Extent of School Desegregation in Metropolitan Areas of Michigan." In *The State of Black Michigan, 1992,* ed. Frances Thomas, 41-54. (East Lansing: Urban Affairs Programs, Michigan State University, 1992).

29. Ibid.

30. Ibid.

31. Edward Simpkins, "Disparities in Funding Patterns and Reading Outcomes in Selected Michigan School Districts." In *The State of Black Michigan, 1992*, ed. Frances Thomas, 55-77. (East Lansing: Urban Affairs Programs, Michigan State University, 1992).

32. Ibid.

33. L. Stevens, "The Dilemma of Metropolitan School Desegregation." *Education and Urban Society* 23 (1990): 61-72.

34. Robert D. Bullard, "Urban Infrastructure: Social, Environmental, and Health Risks to African Americans." In *The State of Black America, 1992*, ed. Billy Tidwell, 183-96. (New York: The National Urban League, 1992).

35. Billy J. Tidwell, "Serving the National Interest: A Marshall Plan for America." In: *The State of Black America, 1992*, ed. Billy Tidwell, 11-30. (New York: The National Urban League, 1992).

36. Robert B. Hill, "Urban Redevelopment: Developing Effective Targeting Strategies." In *The State of Black America, 1992*, ed. Billy J. Tidwell, 197-211. (New York: The National Urban League, 1992).

37. Darden, "Choosing Neighbors and Neighborhoods."

38. E.P. Wolfe, *Trial and Error: The Detroit School Segregation Case.* (Detroit: Wayne State University Press, 1981).

39. Darden, Duleep, and Galster, "Civil Rights in Metropolitan America."

40. George Galster, "Audits Show Racial Discrimination Still Severe in 1980s." *Trends in Housing* 27, no. 6 (1989): 3, 12.

IV.
Education Policy

Assessing Educational Outcomes: Trends and Opportunites

Phyllis T. H. Grummon

WHY ASSESSMENT?

The 1970s and 1980s brought the harsh realization that the United States could no longer count on business as usual in world markets. Other countries, in Asia and Europe, were not only more productive, but also produced more desirable, higher quality goods and services. As policymakers, business, and labor leaders looked at the keys to competitiveness in other countries, it became clear that, along with other factors, the educational systems of our rivals provided a significant advantage. Their educational systems were structured in ways that promoted business interests while also serving the needs of the individual. Some of the educational structures used in these countries include:

- widespread use of apprenticeship and other programs for smooth transitions to the work force;
- national educational systems;
- frequent interchanges/partnerships between businesses and educational institutions on the skill needs of businesses at all levels;
- national workforce training and retraining systems; and
- national standards for educational performance.

These structures combine to create coherent policies on how to best meet the needs of businesses for the initial, and continuing, education and training of the labor force. While all of these structures, and others not mentioned here, are significant, this article focuses on the use of national standards, and assessment of those standards, as a tool for contributing to global competitiveness.

A note of caution here, assessment cannot do the job alone. All of the assessing in the world will be ineffective if schools do not have the understanding and the resources to educate students in the knowledge and skills being assessed. Assessment of student outcomes must be part of broader efforts to restructure school management and curriculum and instruction. Assessment cannot and must not drive the system. Instead, it must be part of an integrated approach to help schools work with all pupils to create the outcomes that society needs.

Before proceeding with a description of the present initiatives and practices in the state and country, it is worthwhile noting the differences between testing and assessment. American students are the most tested in the world. They routinely receive batteries of tests designed to provide information on their achievement levels. By and large these tests consist of multiple choice questions for which there is one right answer. More and more educators and policymakers are beginning to understand that extensive testing has not improved teaching, learning, or elevated outcomes for students.[1]

Assessment, unlike testing, is viewed as part of the process of instruction. It uses a variety of techniques, such as portfolios, performances, essays, student projects, and problem solving exercises, to produce a picture of a student's strengths and weaknesses. Assessments are better able to address student performance in such skill areas as critical thinking, writing and speaking, problem solving, and interpersonal interactions. These are the types of skills that businesses say they must have to remain competitive.[2] The primary criticisms of assessments are that they are lengthy, costly, and do not have the same history of use, which affects their ability to consistently and accurately reflect student achievement, either individually or among students.

KEY POLICY QUESTIONS

There are two key policy issues at stake in the assessment arena.
* Standards—in what areas and at what levels should standards be set
* Assessment vs. Tests—how should achievement of standards be determined

The issues surrounding standards are many. Determining the areas in which standards should be set is the first issue that must be addressed. Should standards cover only basic subjects, such as English and mathematics, or should they be broader to reflect the more complex needs of competitive businesses? Most often, states or localities start with standards in basic subject areas. However, if the future needs of businesses are to be met, then more diverse skills need to be assessed. Surveys of businesses routinely indicate that personal qualities and teamwork skills are as needed in employees as the 3Rs.[3]

Just as important as where standards should be applied, is the level at which standards are set. Setting high standards reflects the belief that everyone can and must achieve at those levels. However, high standards can be politically untenable when it becomes apparent that the majority of students cannot achieve them. Should standards be set low and gradually raised? Finally, the realization of standards depends upon how local districts and individual teachers interpret them in the daily management of instruction. Without careful planning, professional development, and continuing support, even the best standards cannot be met in the classroom.

The second issue, one alluded to above, is to decide what mix of assessment methods and tests is appropriate for determining if students have reached the established standards. Multiple choice tests are a time-honored and accepted means of establishing levels of achievement in individuals. They lend themselves to both sorting students by level, or measuring them to a common standard. They have proven themselves, by and large, to be valid (able to accurately measured) and reliable (able to replicate results over time). However, multiple choice tests are not very effective at determining students' ability to solve complex problems or apply knowledge in either educational or work settings. Being able to add columns of numbers does not guarantee that someone can use math to solve work-related problems.

As defined here, assessment includes a variety of techniques beyond multiple choice tests. Some examples of the methods included under assessment are: extended answer or essay questions, portfolios of work collected over time, computer adaptive testing, interactive video assessment, and ratings of actual performances on tasks as viewed by expert judges. These techniques allow the review of skills not easily tapped in multiple choice tests. Watching someone work in a team to solve a problem provides information that could never be captured by asking a student to select the "best" way to interact in a group from a list of four options. The same can be said for reviewing writing samples from across the curriculum and across time. Assessment methods offer a richer picture of the student's capabilities.

While assessment methodology lends itself more readily to gathering data on diverse skills, it too has drawbacks. First, it is more costly and more time consuming than multiple choice tests. This may be a trade-off that needs to be made in order to gain rich information, but it is not the only obstacle to be overcome. Deciding who to have rate essays, portfolios, or performances is another decision point. Generally that involves determining whether to do ratings locally or centrally. Again, there are advantages and disadvantages for both. Local ratings can take into account differences in curriculum and locally designated outcomes. They also provide teachers with insights into local students which may have more immediate and direct effects on instruction. However, ensuring uniform and fair rating is much more difficult when it is done locally, rather than centrally. Central scoring is also generally less expensive since the number of raters who must be trained is reduced and it can often be contracted out.

The issue of who does the ratings is related to one of the most difficult problems in the general use of assessment methods—ensuring that assessments are both valid and reliable. The first set of problems arise in defining what is meant by some of these skills. For example, there are probably as many ways to "operationalize" a definition for scientific problem solving as there are science teachers. In addition, simply because a task appears on the surface to be assessing scientific problem solving, does not mean that one can accurately predict future scientific problem solving or problem solving in a different area.[4] Without consistent definitions and ways to ensure that similar performances are rated similarly, it will be difficult for assessment methods to move forward.

These problems have been overcome in some areas. Sports offers an example where ratings of performance are widely used and accepted as the assessment method. The Advanced Placement exams are another example of an assessment where extended answers are scored nationally and accepted nationally as judgment of a student's college-level competence in a variety of subject areas. Portfolios have also been widely used in the fields of art, architecture, and writing. However, the breadth of uses anticipated for these assessment methods, and the large number of students who would participate, call for extensive research to ensure any methods used are valid and reliable.

MICHIGAN: THE CURRENT STATE OF ASSESSMENT

Michigan has a long history of developing and using innovative tests and assessments.[5] Early in the Michigan Educational Assessment Program (MEAP), the move was made from norm-referenced (students are ranked on a continuum and judged against each other) to criterion-referenced tests. This means that Michigan students are judged individually on how well they have attained a common set of objectives developed with the help of Michigan teachers. Each student learns how well s/he has learned, and is able to apply, the knowledge gained through instruction. Such tests mean that every student could get "100 percent" by attaining all of the objectives. In addition, the form and substance of the MEAP tests in reading and mathematics have served as models for many other states' assessment programs. The MEAP test in math has worked to incorporate items and strategies relevant to work force readiness. Students are tested in 4th, 7th, and 10th grade in reading and mathematics, and in 5th, 8th, and 11th grade in science. The science test was initiated in 1989.

Aside from the MEAP, most local school districts administer some form of standardized, norm-referenced tests or national criterion-referenced tests. These vary from district to district, but one can find results from such tests as the Iowa Test of Basic Skills, the California Achievement Test, the Differential Aptitudes Test, or the Metropolitan Achievement Test. These tests offer districts the ability to compare their students with a national population of test takers. Local districts may also be using one or more of the assessment methodologies listed above. Portfolios are being more widely used in a number of areas from writing to employability skills. Some districts are also experimenting with performance assessments.

A variety of interests take part in the development and determination of what tests or assessments are used in Michigan. Certainly, local districts are key players. The Michigan Department of Education, through the MEAP and its curriculum and instruction area, also plays a central role. In the past few years, businesses have taken a greater interest in what instruction is delivered and how skills are assessed. A Governor's Task Force on Employability Skills and a State Board of Education Advisory Group on Employability Skills have included business and labor leaders with educators to determine how best to help students develop and assess the skills needed in the Michigan work force. Higher education also plays a role in setting the assessment agenda for K-12 districts.

The legislature, too, plays a significant role, and more so in the recent past. They authorized the legislation for the development and administration of the MEAP in the 1970s. Through Public Act 25 of 1990 the legislature mandated that each district adopt a core curriculum with identified outcomes. Those outcomes must be assessed and reported to community members in the district through an annual report. One of the outcome areas is in employability skills. Section 21-3 of the state aid act to education requires the Department of Education to develop, and the State Board to approve, an employability skills assessment. Presently, an Employability Skills Portfolio has been piloted as the assessment and it is anticipated that it will be adopted by the board as the employability skills assessment.[6]

The state aid act to education of 1991(Public Act 118, Subsection 7) mandates the development of a plan for providing and maintaining a portfolio for each pupil (Section 104). The portfolio would be given to students upon graduation or when leaving the district and would include, at a minimum, all of the following categories of records:

• annual academic and nonacademic plans
• record of academic achievement (e.g., transcripts, test results)
• record of career preparation
• record of recognitions and accomplishments (may be submitted by the student for activities outside of school)

There is considerable overlap between the categories described in Section 104 and the categories included in the proposed Employability Skills Portfolio for Section 21-3, with the latter being more inclusive.

Section 104 a. of that same act requires that districts "award a state-endorsed high school diploma to a pupil scheduled to graduate in 1994, 1995, or 1996 only if the pupil achieves at least 1 of the following:

• a passing score on a locally developed and state-approved basic proficiency test

- a passing score on the general education development test (G.E.D.) for eligible pupils
- achieves at least category 2 on the 10th grade MEAP reading test, at least 50 percent of the objectives on the 10th grade MEAP mathematics test, and at least 50 percent of the objectives on the 11th grade MEAP science test

Further, the legislation mandated that the Department of Education develop, no later than 31 July 1993, and the State Board approve, assessment instruments to determine pupil proficiency in communication skills, mathematics, science, and other subject areas specified by the State Board. These assessment instruments would be given to pupils beginning in 1997 and "a pupil shall not receive a high school diploma unless the pupil achieves passing scores on the assessment instruments developed under this section." In effect, the legislature has mandated a graduation test.

POLICY OPTIONS

The premise that began this piece was the perceived need for different standards and their assessment which has arisen from a clear-cut need for increased global competitiveness. Standards were seen as one method for ensuring that America's work-force would be as able to produce quality goods and services as any in the world. The policy questions described above, concerning standards and tests vs. assessments, are reflected in the issues that policymakers need to discuss about the specifics of assessment in Michigan. For the purposes of discussing the policy options, the standards questions are best subsumed under the question of tests vs. assessments. Since the Michigan legislature has, in effect, proposed both a test and an assessment method to address the needs of business for quality workers, a better framing of that question may be: what roles can and should tests and assessments play? In the sections below, the issues and options, as well as the experiences of other states, related to the graduation proficiency test and the portfolio assessments, will be discussed.

GRADUATION PROFICIENCY TEST

It is not possible to discuss all of the issues related to the development and implementation of a graduation proficiency test.[7] Some of the more salient issues related to legal challenges, standard setting, and national testing will be reviewed. The concept of graduation proficiency tests is not new to Michigan, and a number of other states have enacted such tests with mixed results. Florida, one of the first, had its test subjected to scrutiny by the Supreme Court in the case of *Debra P. v. Turlington*. The finding from that case was that a diploma is a property right and cannot be denied to a student unless it has been adequately demonstrated that the pupil has had an opportunity to learn the material on the test.[8] This finding has an effect on what material can be covered by a graduation test, with the presumption being that a state can only assure that basic subjects have been taught to all pupils. Michigan's legislation proscribes instrument development in communication skills, mathematics, and science and other subject areas specified by the State Board. It would seem wise to limit the inclusiveness of the test, based on *Debra v. Turlington*.

The use of the test by businesses as a "guarantee" of competitive workers may also be limited by legal challenges. A number of Supreme Court and EEOC rulings make it clear that tests used for employment decisions must have documented the use of the skills on the specific job and that better test scores are directly related to better job performance.[9] While the legislation makes no mention, nor should it, of the use of such a test for hiring, it is hard to imagine businesses not requesting applicants to have state-endorsed diplomas. So, the goal of using standards, and tests of how well students meet those standards, to improve competitiveness may not be able to be met directly by a graduation proficiency test.

As potentially contentious as the issue of what areas to test, is the level at which to set the pass/no pass score. As discussed above, the competitive argument would call for setting relatively high scores. Unfortunately, legislators and school districts soon hear from angry students and parents when many students fail to meet those standards. Rationales for how and why standards are set where they are, must be carefully thought out and legally defensible, particularly against charges of bias—not a quick or easy task. Provisions must also be made to give pupils the opportunity to take the proficiency test as often as necessary and to provide them with remediation should they fail to pass. Such steps add considerable expense to a testing program.

While the development and ongoing administration of a graduation proficiency test is expensive, it is something that other states have undertaken. Clearly, there is also pressure at the national level for the development of national tests and assessments of both basic and workforce-ready skill levels. The National Assessment of Educational

Progress (NAEP) has been providing a national "report card" on the levels of literacy among youth and adults for a number of years. However, NAEP does not report scores at the individual level and there are no stakes for students, teachers or individual schools. Several large testing companies—including American College Testing, Educational Testing Service, and the College Entrance Examination Board—are developing assessment systems to try to determine basic and workforce readiness levels. The National Council on Education Standards and Testing believes that national standards and a "system of assessments, measuring progress toward the standards" should be implemented.[10] The amount of attention being focused on the development of national standards, tests, and assessments would seem to imply that at some point in the future there may be a national test or assessment system. The more experience Michigan has in the development and administration of its own system, the better it will be able to inform national developments and to implement national measures.

PORTFOLIO ASSESSMENTS

Aside from a graduation proficiency test, Michigan has been pursuing the development of portfolios as an assessment method. While other states—such as Vermont, Kentucky, and California—are also working with portfolios, they all tend to be focusing more narrowly in specific subject areas and not broadly on work force readiness or employability. Thus, Michigan is in the more or less enviable position of being ahead of the rest of the nation in this area. Up to this point, only the piloting of the Employability Skills Portfolio (approximately 10,000 pupils have participated) and school district planning for the Section 104 portfolio have occurred. In the 1993-94 school year it is likely that many districts will be implementing the Employability Skills Portfolio as a way to comply with Section 104. Since the Employability Skills Portfolio had been piloted and supported by the department, it has gained widespread acceptance.

Many of the general issues described for assessment methods apply to the portfolios under consideration in Michigan. One of those issues is how to define the material to be included in a portfolio. Section 104 identifies specifically the categories of information to be included. In contrast, the Employability Skills Portfolio includes definitions for skills, as developed by the Employability Skills Task Force, and offers guidelines for determining what evidence might be included to indicate that a skill has been attained. It is also possible for local districts to include additional skills and their associated evidence in ES Portfolios. For example, local businesses may wish to contribute those skills they see as important for work force readiness. As such, the ES Portfolio takes on an outcomes orientation, which is in keeping with the intent of Public Act 25 and the Core Curriculum.

The issue of who should help review portfolio contents will also have to be resolved. Presently, students in most Employability Skills pilot districts are responsible for maintaining their portfolios, so the cost in staff time has not been great. However, to be meaningful to pupils, portfolios should be reviewed by either educational staff or businesses. This will require a greater time investment. The issue of cost has had some, but not complete, resolution. At this point, the cost of the physical portfolio has been kept to a minimum. However, as benchmarks are developed and portfolios begin to be rated, the costs may rise dramatically. The Department of Education staff are presently working on setting benchmarks or standards for reviewing portfolio contents. Without them, the portfolio may lose its impact on students. It is most likely that a series of standards will be set to allow pupils to see progress. How portfolios will ultimately be used for instructional and assessment purposes is not completely clear. Neither is how students might use them as they enter the job market or seek entry to college.

A number of additional issues, while having been resolved in the local districts piloting the ES Portfolio, have not been decided statewide. By and large, the ES portfolio has been seen as student owned and managed, although Section 104 requires the school to take responsibility for portfolios. Most districts have provided storage space for the ES portfolios, but students have been largely responsible for determining what is kept in them. The issue of storage implies not only the logistics of physical space, but also that of access. The Family Educational Right to Privacy Act (FERPA) and the Hatch amendment both have implications for who can have access to potentially sensitive student records. Schools need to consider how they will store portfolios and allow students access to them, while ensuring they are secure from unauthorized access. Transfer of portfolios with students must also be documented and occur on a timely basis.

CONCLUSIONS

As states face the reality of global competitiveness and the likelihood of national educational standards, they must make decisions about what and how to assess their students. While this article has focused on those issues for the K-12 student population, they will be no less salient for adult education, alternative educational settings, and even special education. Within the framework presented here, policymakers face choices in a number of areas. These choices pertain to:

- Standards—in what areas, and at what levels, should standards be set, and
- Assessment vs. Tests—how should achievement of standards be determined.

Policymakers need to keep clearly in mind the purposes for any standards and their associated assessments or tests. If, for example, the purpose of proposing a standard for graduation is to assure better entry-level workers, then assessments or tests need to be designed with that goal in mind. The level at which standards will be set and the areas in which students must meet standards should be associated with the actual needs of businesses. It must also be determined whether schools and the state are able to judge students as meeting those standards, or if that should be left to businesses. Policymakers may decide that the purpose of standards is to ensure that students have met certain levels of proficiency in designated subject matter areas, regardless of whether or not those are needed past high school graduation. This purpose would call for a different set of standards, levels of attainment, and subject area foci. In short, before deciding what standards, what levels, and what assessment tools, policymakers must be clear about what they hope those standards will accomplish for the greater social good.

At present, it is not clear which purposes policymakers hope to accomplish with standards setting and assessment. Rather, Michigan is presently looking at specific test and assessment options. Both a high stakes graduation proficiency test and a low stakes portfolio assessment process are presently in legislation. The standards for an endorsed diploma, at least for the next three years, have been mandated by legislation. The standards by which portfolios will be judged are still being developed. The subject areas for review for the graduation proficiency test have not been determined. Those for the

Employability Skills Portfolio have been developed through interactions with business, labor, and education. Michigan's strategy to pursue both a test and an assessment may prove useful in the national arena as it allows Michigan to have input into both camps as national development on standards is pursued.

There are drawbacks to developing each method. The primary drawback for the graduation proficiency test is the considerable expense associated with its development. Such expense may be hard to rationalize in an era of tight resources since the benefits are unknown. States that have implemented graduation tests have not reported any widespread effects on the success of graduates when they pass such tests. In addition, it is most likely that any test developed will face legal challenges, another expense. Setting the cut score for passing may also be difficult. Setting it too low loses the positive effects of guaranteeing prepared students, setting it too high increases the need for remedial work and repeat testing for those who fail. In this age of accountability, it is attractive to be able to say that high school graduates are certified, but policymakers must be sure they are willing to pay the economic and political price of ensuring that through a test.

A portfolio assessment solves some, but not all, of the problems raised for graduation proficiency tests. Implementing the portfolio assessment process appears to be less expensive, and easier to phase in over time. Since it focuses on the development of students through integration into curriculum and instruction, as well as the assessment of their skills, it is also likely to have broader benefits. However, without support from businesses and postsecondary institutions, its usefulness will be diminished. Students will need to be able to measure themselves—and to be measured—against benchmarks, and those benchmarks must be reinforced in the worlds they enter following graduation. The development of valid and reliable benchmarks, even if the portfolio remains low stakes, will take time, effort, and money. Portfolios are not likely to work as a guarantee. As designed now, however, businesses and colleges can review portfolios or parts of them, and make their own determinations of students' preparation. This makes the role of the school and the state not one of certifying students, but one of helping students to certify themselves. The purposes defined by policymakers for standards play a key role in deciding how the graduation proficiency test and the portfolio are ultimately used in Michigan.

NOTES

1. National Commission on Testing and Public Policy, "From Gatekeeper to Gateway: Transforming Testing in America." (Boston College, Chestnut Hill, MA: National Commission on Testing and Public Policy, 1990)
2. Governor's Task Force on Employability Skills, "Report to the Governor's Commission on Jobs and Economic Development," (Lansing, Mich: Governor's Office, April 1988); Secretary's Commission on Achieving Necessary Skills (SCANS), "What Work Requires of Schools: A SCANS Report for America 2000," (Washington, D.C.: U.S. Department of Labor, 1991).
3. W. Mehrens, "Michigan Empoyability Skills Technical Report," November 1989 (Michigan State University, East Lansing, MI); SCANS, "What Work Requires of Schools."
4. G. Wiggins, "Creating Tests Worth Taking," *Educational Leadership* **VOL??** (May 1992): 26-33.
5. Michigan State Board of Education, "Michigan Educational Assessment Program Handbook. (Lansing, Mich: Michigan State Board of Education, 1991-1992).
6. Private communication, State Board Advisory Group on Employability Skills, October 1992.
7. Expert Panel Report to the State Superintendent. (1992). "Issues and Recommendations Regarding Implementation of the Michigan High School Graduation Tests", (Michigan State University, April 1992).
8. *Debra P. v. Turlington*, 564 F. Supp. 177 (M.D. Fla. 1983), *aff'd*, 730 F.2d 1405 (11th Cir. 1984).
9. "Fairness in Employment Testing," *Journal of Vocational Behavior* 33, no. 3 (December 1988).
10. National Council of Education Standards an , "Raising Standards for American Educaiton", (Washington, D.C.: National Council for Education Standards and Testing, January 1992).

School Finance: Finding the Dollars to Make Educational Sense

Ruth Beier

There is no doubt about it—Michigan needs school finance reform. Unfortunately, there is also no doubt that the state and local political structure in Michigan has so far made responsible school finance reform nearly impossible. This chapter examines Michigan's school financing structure, impediments to school finance reform, and arguments for and against different avenues of school reform.

DOES MICHIGAN REALLY NEED SCHOOL FINANCE REFORM?

The following facts indicate that the current school finance system in Michigan is not working:

- Michigan has some of the highest property taxes in the country. Depending on the method of measurement, Michigan property tax levels rank either ninth or tenth highest in the nation.[1] Figure 1 compares per capita property taxes in Michigan to the other Great Lakes states and to two states—Kentucky and Tennessee—which many businesses view as powerful economic competitors.
- In addition to relatively high levels of local property taxes, residential property tax bases (50 percent of the market value of property) in Michigan often increase faster than incomes, making the property tax a growing financial burden for many home owners. As shown in Figure 2, property values have been rising faster than inflation since 1985.[2]

- Students do not have equal access to quality education, and the quality of a child's education depends on the location of that child's home. Some Michigan districts spend $10,000 per student per year, and are considered to have some of the best K-12 programs in the country. Other Michigan districts spend $3,000 per student per year, and cannot afford to offer the education students will need to compete in a technologically advanced society. Recent rejection by voters of property tax increases have resulted in extensive school budget reductions, and an increase in financial stress for poorer school districts. In the most extreme case, the Kalkaska School District (in the northwestern Lower Peninsula) closed its public schools early in 1992 in March—due to lack of funds.
- Home owners in urban areas tend to pay much more in school taxes that those in suburban areas, but urban school districts end up with less revenue per student.

HOW DOES MICHIGAN FINANCE SCHOOLS?

Michigan school revenue is based primarily on local property taxes and state aid, with a small percentage of total funds coming from the federal government. Voters in every school district decide how much to tax themselves for schools by approving school operating millage.[3] There is no minimum voted millage requirement, although the Michigan Constitution sets a maximum local rate of 50 mills.

In addition to the revenue raised by local property taxes, state law guarantees that each district receive a certain amount of revenue per pupil per mill, and sends state aid to school districts that raise less than the guarantee from their own property taxes. School districts with small property tax bases (low SEV) raise little in local property taxes and receive more state aid than school districts with larger property tax bases. (Note that the guarantee does not encourage districts to lower their property tax rates because they are guaranteed more revenue per pupil at higher millage rates.)

Because property-poor school districts receive the most state aid, this type of formula is called a "power equalizing" state aid formula. If the revenue raised by property taxes in a school district is greater than the amount guaranteed by the school aid formula, that school district receives no revenue from the power equalizing formula.

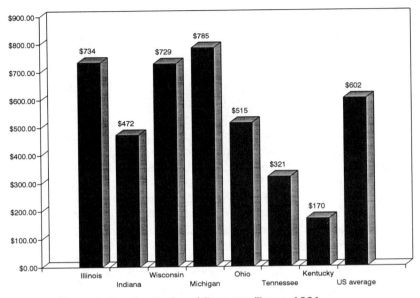

Figure 1. Per Capita Local Property Taxes, 1991

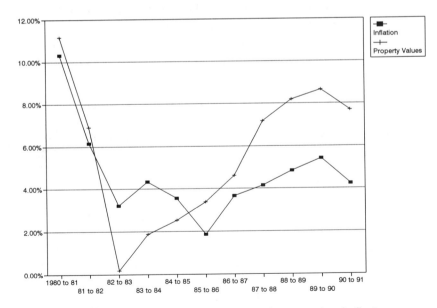

Figure 2. Percentage Increase in Property Taxes Compared to Inflation

Districts that receive formula aid are commonly referred to as "in-formula" districts. Those that receive no formula aid are referred to as "out-of-formula" districts. There are about 170 "out-of-formula" districts and 400 "in-formula" school districts in Michigan.

WHAT'S WRONG WITH THE CURRENT POWER EQUALIZING SYSTEM?

In theory, Michigan's power equalizing school financing system is not flawed. Local residents pay property taxes, and the state supplements this effort so that property-poor districts are not disadvantaged. In practice, Michigan's school finance system does not achieve the goal of fiscal equalization. Property taxes are much higher than the national average and there is a huge disparity in property values and educational opportunities among Michigan public school districts.

The reason the system does not work is simple: *the disparity in property wealth in Michigan is too great to be compensated for by the state-funded power equalizing formula.* In other words, the distribution of property wealth in Michigan is so skewed, it is impossible (at current state tax rates) for the state to spend enough in the property-poor districts to bring them up to the level of the property-rich districts. This school finance problem will exist as long as Michigan maintains current school district boundaries, and property taxes are the major funding source of schools.

EFFECTS OF MICHIGAN'S SCHOOL FINANCE SYSTEM

In addition to the inequity in school funding discussed above, Michigan's school finance system has led to detrimentally high urban millage rates and a shift in the school finance burden from the state to local property taxes.

URBAN MILLAGE RATES ARE TOO HIGH

Michigan's school finance system forces urban areas with declining property values (such as Detroit, Flint, and Saginaw) to increase property tax rates to keep school revenue from declining, while growing suburban areas have been able to keep rates down and still see property tax revenues rise. For example, Detroit now levies about 90 mills (after state aid) and receives \$4,000 per student; while suburban Bloomfield Hills levies about 24 mills and receives \$8,000 per student.

Extremely high urban millage rates further encourage investment in lower-taxes suburban areas, increasing the disparity in property values, and putting even more pressure on cities to raise their millage rates.

STATE AID IS TOO LOW

Another problem with Michigan's school finance system is that rising property values have allowed the state to reduce its commitment to schools. Because the state simply supplements local property tax revenue, when property tax revenue increases, state funding responsibility falls. As shown in Exhibit 3, this is exactly what has happened in the past ten years in Michigan. Growing SEV's have allowed the state to reduce its portion of school financing. This shift in burden from state tax sources to local property taxes has increased the disparity in school funding.

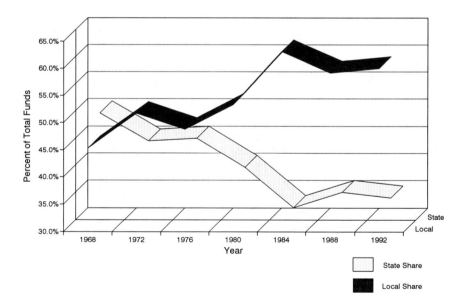

Figure 3. Percent of Total K-12
Revenue from State and Local Sources

THE SYSTEM BECOMES MORE PRECARIOUS EACH YEAR

Only about 35 percent of the households in Michigan have children in K-12 schools, and this percentage will decline as the Michigan population continues to grow older on average. This demographic shift makes it more likely local millage elections will fail, as fewer and fewer families receive direct benefits from primary education.

WHY HAS SCHOOL FINANCE REFORM NOT HAPPENED?

There have been three major impediments to school finance reform over the past ten years.

1. The state cannot afford to significantly reduce disparity among existing school districts without increasing taxes, unless high spending districts are forced to reduce spending.

Few policymakers interested in reforming school financing support reducing spending in richer districts to achieve equity. The most common argument against this strategy is that it is not appropriate to reduce educational opportunities in some areas in order to achieve equity. Raising state revenue is an option, although it may be as politically unappealing as reducing revenue in high spending districts. Following are major revenue-raising options.

- Raising the sales tax rate. The state sales tax rate is limited by the Constitution, and can be increased only with a vote of the people. In past years, every ballot proposal that would have shifted school funding from property taxes to the sales tax has failed.
- Broadening the sales tax base. The sales tax base could be broadened significantly without amending the constitution. For example, under current law, all services are exempt from taxation. Taxing services could raise up to $4 billion per year, depending on the number of services included.[4]
- Raising the income tax rate. The state income tax rate of 4.6 percent is near the national average for states that have income taxes. The state constitution prohibits a graduated rate structure, so a rate increase would have to apply to all taxpayers. Michigan's income tax base is already very broad, and there are few opportunities for increasing revenue by further base-broadening.

- Raising the single business tax (SBT) rate. The Michigan SBT is a 2.35 percent tax on the value a business adds to the product or service it produces, with some exemptions and deductions. The base of the SBT is much broader than the business tax base in any other state. Small increases in the tax rate would result in significant increases in revenue. Many Michigan businesses argue that the SBT is already too burdensome, particularly in low-profit years.

2. *Local school districts and many local residents fight school reforms that reduce local control over tax revenue and spending. This includes plans that raise statewide taxes in order to reduce local property taxes or plans to consolidate school districts.*

Following are the "local control" arguments most often heard in discussing school finance reform proposals.

- The property tax millage is the only rate on which residents get to vote. Residents who want to spend more for education can approve higher millage rates, with very little interference from the state. There is concern, especially in high-spending districts, that replacing the property tax with a statewide tax would make it impossible for some districts to spend as much as residents are willing to pay on schools.

There are two common responses to this local control argument. First, property taxes increase without voter-approved millage increases because residential property values tend to rise every year. And second, because the state has reduced its commitment to fund education, residents do not really have a choice, and must increase millages in order to maintain education funding.

- Revenue raised and spent locally is used more efficiently than revenue raised statewide and distributed to school districts. School tax revenue buys buildings, supplies, teachers, and administrators; and it does not support a large bureaucracy. In contrast, statewide taxes must first be used to support the state bureaucracy before public goods and services can be purchased.
- Taxpayers do not trust the state to support schools or to distribute school revenue. There are two major reasons for this distrust. First, taxpayers realize that if state revenue is tight and other expenditure needs rise, revenue that was once earmarked for education could be spent elsewhere. An example of this is the state's decision to reduce other state support for schools when the lottery started raising significant amounts of education revenue. Second, many

residents fear the possibility that the state might decide to change the distribution of school funds, harming their particular district.

- Many local residents identify strongly with their local schools, particularly their local high schools. Many proposals to consolidate small school districts have not been able to overcome the desire to maintain local identities. Interestingly, even low-property value school districts most often oppose consolidation proposals that would significantly increase available revenue.

3. *Political gridlock and powerful lobbying have prevented legislative action, so all recent school reform plans have been on the statewide ballot, where their complexity ensures defeat.*

In the past three administrations, Republicans, Democrats, and powerful education lobbying groups have been unable to agree on a school finance reform plan that significantly improves equity in educational financing. As a result, there have been five proposals to reduce property taxes and/or to reform school finances placed on the statewide ballot in the past ten years. All of these proposals have failed, and most voters agree that the ballot is not the proper place for complicated school finance reform plans.[5]

WHAT ARE SOME SCHOOL FINANCE REFORM OPTIONS?

Following is a discussion of three recently debated strategies designed to address the problem of high property taxes and/or school financing.

1. *Cut school property taxes, limit assessment increases, exempt some property from taxation, and do not specifically address school finance reform.*

The recently defeated ballot proposal, Proposal C, is an example of this strategy. Many proposals of this type have been considered by the legislature over the past five years, including proposals to reduce the assessment ratio from 50 percent to 30 percent of market value, to reduce millage rates, and to exempt a percentage of property from school taxes.

ARGUMENTS FOR

A. This type of plan would significantly reduce property taxes in Michigan, bringing the state more in line with the national average.

B. An assessment limitation would hold residential property tax burden as a percentage of income relatively constant.
C. A property tax exemption would be the most progressive option.

ARGUMENTS AGAINST

A. This type of plan would address the problem of high property taxes, but would do nothing to improve educational equity.
B. Unless other revenue sources are used to replace property taxes, this type of plan would reduce revenue available for schools.

2. *Cut school property taxes, and replace lost revenue with a statewide tax and/or other local taxes.*

The proposal now being considered by a bipartisan school finance legislative working group (the Team 11 Plan) is an example of this strategy.

ARGUMENTS FOR

A. This type of plan would significantly reduce property taxes in Michigan, bringing the state more in line with the national average.
B. It could reduce school district funding disparities by increasing reliance on state-raised and state-distributed sources.
C. It could allow local districts to raise taxes to increase expenditures above the amount provided by the increased state taxes.
D. Because it would not refund school districts dollar for dollar for property tax revenue losses, it would not result in the state spending scarce resources to maintain an inequitable funding system.

ARGUMENTS AGAINST

A. The state tax increases needed to fund this type of proposal are significant. For example, the Team 11 proposal calls for an increase in the personal income tax rate from 4.6 percent to 7.25 percent and an increase in the SBT rate from 2.35 percent to 5.8 percent.
B. School districts that are wealthy because of the existence of commercial and industrial property would lose revenue, unless

voters approve increases in other local taxes (in the Team 11 proposal, a school district income tax.) Residents in these areas may have chosen their home location precisely because they were able to export some of their school tax burden to local businesses, and may be unwilling to tax themselves to the extent needed to maintain current funding levels.

C. This type of plan would reduce local control.

D. If property tax revenue is replaced dollar for dollar by some state source, the state would, in effect, be using scarce resources to support an inequitable system.

3. *Modify the current system to reduce disparity and selectively reduce property taxes in high tax rate or low-income areas.*

The Olmstead/Kearny school finance reform plan is an example of this type of proposal. Under this plan, low-spending school districts would receive more formula aid and school districts with high millage rates and low SEV would be further rewarded through the school aid formula for reducing millages. This plan could be implemented to the extent that the state could fund it, with or without a tax increase.

ARGUMENTS FOR

A. This plan would reduce millage rates in urban areas, and reduce the incentive for businesses and home owners to live outside of center cities.

B. It would increase school funding to low-spending school districts, improving school district funding equity.

C. It does not decrease local control.

ARGUMENTS AGAINST

A. Without a tax increase, the state may not be able to fund the formula enough to make a difference in millage rates or in school funding.

B. This type of plan does not address the issues of high property taxes and rising assessment levels in the suburbs.

SUMMARY

Michigan needs school finance reform that addresses the dual problems of high property taxes and disparity in spending among local school districts. The avenue to school reform is strewn with obstacles, including the desire for local control, political gridlock, state budget limitations, and voter distrust. In order to overcome these obstacles, the state legislature and the governor must agree on a school finance reform plan that can be approved in the legislature and not be placed on the ballot.

NOTES

1. See United States Advisory Commission on Intergovernmental Relations, 1991, *Significant Features of Fiscal Federalism.*
2 See the *United States Consumer Price Index.* Property value data is from the Michigan Department of Treasury, Lansing, Michigan.
3. One "mill" is equal to .001 dollars. In Michigan, property taxes are calculated by multiplying millage by SEV (state equalized value of property), where SEV is equal to 50 percent of the market value of property. For example, the owner of an $80,000 home ($40,000 SEV) with a school millage of 35 pays $40,000 * .035, or $1,400 each year in school taxes.
4. These districts do receive some state aid in areas such as transportation, social security, and special education, although the amount distributed for this type of "categorical aid" has been shrinking in recent years as the state has looked for ways to balance the budget.
5. Calculated from *1990 Census of Service Industries,* U.S. Department of Commerce Geographic Area Series, Washington, D.C.: Government Printing Office.
6. The only property tax ballot proposal that has been approved by voters in recent years, the tax limitation amendment of 1978, had little effect on disparity in school financing.

V.
Health Policy
in Michigan

Health Care Reform in Michigan: Problems, Policies, and Prospects

Carol S. Weissert, Andrew J. Hogan, and Leonard M. Fleck

Health care reform has been the focus of dozens of political campaigns, state legislative sessions, association conferences, and academic treatises. The problems prompting these efforts are real. Taxpayers worry about possibly losing their health insurance, and businesses complain about the rising costs of providing those insurance benefits. Providers and insurance companies are concerned about their current financial viability and what effect possible changes could have on how they do business. State governments and Washington see more and more of their spending choices narrowed as health care costs consume larger and larger shares of public budgets.

For some, experts and the public alike, national health insurance is imminent; others are less certain—pointing out that the issue has been on the national agenda, off and on, for over half a century. Even if there is national reform, the question of the state role remains pertinent. Are the states to be players in any national debate, highlighting experiences and concerns relevant to their constituents? Will states continue to be major partners in the provision of health care and the regulation of providers and insurers? Will the states continue to forge the way on their own? States have been active in the past several years, launching both major and incremental reforms to improve access, hold down costs, reform the small business insurance market, and control medical malpractice. Michigan, too, has studied and enacted programs to improve access and control health care costs.

The question before the Michigan legislature in 1993 is whether it can make a contribution toward health care system reform, and if so, how. This chapter provides some guidance in considering these questions. It sets out the key policy questions before Michigan and other states, outlines the importance of the issue to Michigan, briefly describes options available and the experiences of other states, and presents some modest principles that legislators interested in health care reform might wish to consider.

KEY POLICY QUESTIONS

WHAT CAN BE DONE ABOUT THE COST OF HEALTH CARE AND ITS RAMPANT GROWTH?

The U.S. health care system is the costliest in the world. In 1991, total U.S. expenditures for health care were $740 billion or about 13.2 percent of the nation's Gross National Product (GNP). By 1995, health spending is expected to total $1.1 trillion or 15 percent of our GNP. By way of comparison, in 1991 Canada and virtually all the nations of Europe were spending less than 10 percent of their GNP on health care.

The rate of increase in health care spending is far outstripping the growth in income in the U.S. compared to other countries. Between 1975 and 1989, total health expenditures as a percent of GDP (Gross Domestic Product) grew 40 percent in the United States, compared to growth rates of 21 percent in Canada, 24 percent in France, 5 percent in the United Kingdom, and 0 percent in Germany.[1] These differentials are due to the low rate of GDP growth in the United States combined with continued high levels of health spending.

WHAT CAN BE DONE TO PROVIDE HEALTH CARE FOR EVERYONE WHO NEEDS IT?

The number of Americans without any health insurance has grown constantly since the mid-1970s, now totaling more than 35 million. Some three-fourths of these are employed, or are dependents of employed individuals, who are working in low-wage jobs to which health benefits are not provided. When these uninsured persons require medical care, they are more subject to denial or provision of lower quality care than those "covered" by insurance.[2] Lack of health insurance coverage is a major cause of personal bankruptcy in the United States.

HOW CAN WE ASSURE THAT THE DOLLARS GO TO IMPROVE OUR HEALTH?

Even though we have the most expensive health care system in the world, we are collectively no better off in health status or length of life than countries that spend substantially less on health care. Some evidence suggests that much of the additional spending in the United States reflects unnecessary care, excess capacity, and administrative costs that do not improve health.[3]

HOW CAN WE DEAL WITH THE COMPLEXITY AND INTERRELATEDNESS OF THE HEALTH CARE SYSTEM?

Efforts made to "clamp down" on one aspect of the health system often fail or result in unintended consequences on other aspects. For example, when taxpayers want to reduce spending for publicly funded health programs—notably Medicaid—states must often reduce payments to hospitals and physicians who care for those patients and/or raise eligibility standards so that fewer persons qualify for the program. In either case, when the poor get sick, they must then go to hospitals which provide "charity" or free care. However, the care is not really free, but is paid for by shifting the uncompensated costs on insured patients through higher charges. Another example is the use of caps or limits on physician fees as a way to control costs. However, as long as physicians can see more patients, provide more extensive services as a way of recouping their losses, or bill separately for services previously provided as a package, few savings accrue. Finally, insurance market reforms designed to enable more persons to be covered can result in more businesses taking on insurance risks or "self-insuring" to avoid state requirements under exemptions provided in the Employee Retirement Income Security Act of 1974 (ERISA).

HOW CAN WE BE RESPONSIVE TO THE PUBLIC DEMANDS FOR UP-TO-DATE HEALTH TECHNOLOGY AND STILL HOLD DOWN COSTS?

We have known for some time that one of the primary causes of health care cost escalation is deployment of new and expensive medical technologies. Yet curbs on the acquisition of these technologies,

through Certificate of Need (CON) requirements and other constraints, often run into intense opposition by hospitals that feel they
cannot be competitive without the most up-to-date technology.
Citizens also may oppose such cost-saving requirements, feeling it is
their right to have access—and in a convenient location—to these
technologies, such as magnetic resonance imaging (MRI), or angio-
plasty, or bone marrow transplantation when they need it.

HOW CAN A STATE DEAL WITH THIS MASSIVE PROBLEM WHEN THE FEDERAL GOVERNMENT IS A KEY ACTOR AS WELL?

One major public insurance program—Medicare—is fully federally
controlled; and another—Medicaid—is a joint federal-state program
with Washington demanding more and more expansions in recent
years. Federal law setting forth national requirements on pension and
health care programs, ERISA, has become a major impediment to
change at the state level since it exempts self-insured health plans
(those where the business or firm assumes the risks for health care
costs) from state requirements imposed upon health insurance companies. Fully 50 percent of the nation's workers with private insurance are enrolled in these self-insured plans. Further, any state
wishing to deviate from Medicaid requirements must receive a federal
"waiver" to proceed. While one of the most innovative state efforts to
reform its health system, Oregon's health care "rationing" plan was
recently granted such a federal waiver, the process took several years
and the waiver was originally denied.

WHY IS HEALTH CARE REFORM AN IMPORTANT ISSUE IN MICHIGAN

MICHIGAN'S CADILLAC EXPECTATIONS ON CHEVROLET REALITIES

In the 1960s, Michigan established health care consumption patterns that were above the national average, and they have continued
to grow at national rates. Michigan's per capita health care costs are
$2,569—about 9 percent more than the national average.

In the past, the state enjoyed above-average income based on substantial manufacturing employment. Today, however, Michigan's per
capita income, having risen more slowly than the country's as a
whole, falls near the U.S. average. In the last decade, median per

capita family income and real income from wages and salaries fell in Michigan. The growing divergence between health expenditures, and income to support them, has led to a health care affordability crisis for both the public and private sectors in the state, which is at least as acute as in the nation as a whole.

The sluggish income growth has adversely affected state coffers as well. The traditional sources of public revenue in Michigan, the sales tax, the personal income tax, and the single business tax, are all tied to personal income and earnings. The state's ability to finance the cost of health care (for the poor as well as its own employees) is therefore limited by the slow growth in earnings among much of its working population.

The single largest health expenditure in Michigan's state budget is Medicaid, which at over $2 billion makes up slightly over half of the state's total health spending. Spending on Michigan's Medicaid program doubled during the 1980s, even though the enrollment remained relatively flat. State expenditures for others for whom it provides health care—active employees, state government retirees, and public school retirees—quadrupled, sextupled, and octupled, respectively over the same period. In the long run, none of these expenditure growth rates can be sustained.

COST-SHIFTING WEAKENS ACCOUNTABILITY

Michigan, like most states, has attempted to control its largest health expenditure—Medicaid—by paying health care providers for their services at less than market rates and by reducing coverage for the non-disabled poor. In response, health care providers have engaged in a practice called "cost-shifting," by which the bills of private pay patients are augmented to offset unreimbursed costs from Medicaid and uninsured patients. As evidence of this practice, we note that the state health expenditures on behalf of state employees have increased at twice the rate of Medicaid expenditures.

Cost-shifting represents as much as 30 percent of the increase in the cost of private health insurance. As the cost of private coverage escalates, due to the combination of cost-shifting and medical inflation, low-wage employers and employees will drop coverage. During the late 1980s, lack of health insurance became increasingly common, in spite of sustained economic growth and falling unemployment. With the recession and sustained economic stagnation of the early 1990s, the pressures on the health system have accelerated, abetted by growing welfare rolls and the increase in health care utilization, which accompanies most economic downturns.

"HIDDEN" TAX SUBSIDIES FURTHER WEAKENS ACCOUNTABILITY

Tax subsidies for employee health benefits reduce the sensitivity of patients to health care cost inflation. Employees have little incentive to resist extravagant health benefits for which employers can deduct the costs from their tax liability. Tax subsidies lead to revenue losses for the state budget. In Michigan, losses attributable to the health insurance tax subsidy total nearly $1 billion. In addition, cost-shifting accentuates tax expenditure losses since insurance premiums rise, eroding the revenue base for the Medicaid program, and inducing further underfunding, more uninsurance, and ultimately more cost-shifting. The mutually reinforcing nature of cost-shifting and tax expenditures virtually guarantees the long-run unsustainability of Medicaid, barring a very substantial growth in per capita income and corresponding state revenues.

The United States' (and Michigan's) health system is almost by any measure unfair and growing more unfair as its financial instability increases. Apart from the moral challenge presented by a system that subsidizes the health insurance premiums of the rich while eliminating Medicaid benefits for the working poor, the growing awareness of the current inequities undermines public support for the health system.

GETTING OUR MONEY'S WORTH

In spite of the staggering monetary commitment that the country and Michigan have made to providing health care, the system's performance in achieving public health goals can only be judged poor. While Michigan spends some $20 billion in total (public and private) health care expenses, it compares unfavorably with other states in both infant mortality and preventable chronic disease. Michigan has the highest death rates from chronic disease in the United States (483 per 100,000 population), and infant mortality rates exceed the national average.

THE PUBLIC'S (MIS)PERCEPTION

Although most Americans, and most Michiganians, are happy with the personal health services they receive, they often express concerns with issues of system efficacy and cost. Further, many Americans who currently have private health insurance are experiencing a growing anxiety about their continuing ability to afford health insurance and the protection it provides from medical catastrophe. The percentage of Americans dissatisfied with their own health care increased from 13 percent in 1987, to 26 percent in 1992.[4] While increasing numbers of citizens are willing to consider a government-run insurance plan like that in Canada and some European countries, distrust for government programs, especially relating to their cost and efficacy, is widespread and growing. At the same time, many accept the axiom that "health care is different," making purely market-based solutions infeasible.

The Public Agenda Foundation recently reported that the general public's perception of the health care system is based on rather simplistic notions of provider inefficiency and administrative waste by insurance carriers. Experts, on the other hand, argue that the problems are more fundamental and that solutions will require sacrifice from the consuming public, including consideration of rationing of health services. The divergence in opinion between the public and expert perceptions of the current health system and how it can be reformed has contributed to the seemingly interminable reports of study groups, panels, commissions, and task forces as well as the proliferation of health-related lobbyists in Washington and Lansing.

Political gains can be garnered through these efforts to express concern with the current state of the health system, but recent state efforts to reform the health system have frequently rewarded their proponents with significant political problems. Some states have been successful, although the choices are difficult and the going tough.[5]

POLICY OPTIONS

In the health care arena, the solutions are as well known as the problems. Some deal primarily with cost containment (setting global health budgets); others with improving access (pay or play schemes that encourage businesses to provide health care insurance to their employees). Some are targeted to certain populations (uninsured poor) or particular problem areas (underserved areas of the state); others are more ambitious efforts to evoke fundamental change (single-payor systems). Some are primarily the focus of state actions (small group insurance reforms); others are under consideration at both governmental levels (all-payor systems). Finally, some "stand alone," but most can be adopted in some combination.

The reforms can be roughly grouped into three areas: those that strengthen the public or governmental role; those that strengthen the private health care market, and those that build on the current public-private system in operation today. Table 1 describes policy options within each grouping and outlines the advantages and disadvantages of each policy.

Table 1.
State Health Policy Reforms:
Objectives, Assessments and Examples

A. Strong Governmental Role

Policy	Principal Objective	Description	Advantages/ Disadvantages	Examples
All Payor tSystem	Cost Control	One agency sets common billing, negotiates fees, sets limits on spending/ services	A: Some evidence controls costs and reduces cost shifts D: Hard to set rates and spending ceilings	MD NJ MA NY
Single Payor System (Canadian Plan)	Cost Control	Government provides health care system rather than regulates it	A: May control costs and eliminate cost shifts D: Success in other countries may not apply here	CAN-ADA VT study
Regional Based Approach	Cost Control/ Improving Access	Regional bodies are set up to provide target budget and manage competition	A: Regional bodies can better reflect needs, conditions in certain parts of state D: Hard to set rates and spending ceilings	CA proposed

(continued on next page)

Table 1. *(cont.)*

B. Market-Based Options

Policy	Principal Objective	Description	Advantages/ Disadvantages	Examples
Eliminate Tax Expenditure on Private Health Insurance	Improve Citizen Information	Fully tax value of private health insurance (or tax it above some minimal level)	A: Consumers might make better choices about health insurance. Would also provide more revenues D: Would mean higher taxes for citizens	Proposed at federal level
Provide Tax Credit for low-income families purchasing health insurance	Improve Access	Could require every family to purchase health insurance, giving tax credits only to poor	A: If large enough, might encourage uninsured to buy insurance. D: Would be costly for treasury	
Regulatory Relief	Reduce costs/ improve access	Includes reducing insurance mandates, allowing "bare-bones" policies, loosening requirements on rural hospitals	A: Politically popular, may help both providers, insurers and consumers D: May do little to solve big problems.	Many States

(continued on next page)

Table 1. *(cont.)*

Policy	Principal Objective	Description	Advantages/ Disadvantages	Examples
Small Group Insurance Reform	Improve access	Includes subsidized premiums, risk pooling, small employer buyer groups, community rating	A: Good use of states' regulatory power over insurance companies D. Hard to get small businesses to participate	According to GAO, nearly every state has done something in this area

C. Combining Resources of Public and Private Sector

Policy	Principal Objective	Description	Advantages/ Disadvantages	Examples
State Mandates Providing Universal Access	Improve Access	Requires employers to provide health insurance for workers	A. Deals effectively with large number of otherwise uninsured D. Impossible without ERISA exemption	HI
Pay or Play Plans	Improve Access	Requires employers to provide health insurance to employees or pay a tax to help finance the state's health insurance system	A. Provides strong encouragement for businesses to provide insurance D. May encourage businesses to "self-insure"	OR MA

(continued on next page)

Table 1. *(cont.)*

Policy	Principal Objective	Description	Advantages/ Disadvantages	Examples
State Subsidies of the Uninsured	Improve Access	Provide direct subsidies to uninsured adults and/or low income children	A. Avoids problems with ERISA and getting businesses to act D. Is expensive	WA ME MN
Medicaid Expansions and Buy-In	Improve Access	Expand Medicaid eligibility to low-income children or allow low-income to participate in Medicaid with small premium	A. Builds on existing federal-state program D. Doesn't deal with current problems in Medicaid such as "stigma" and high cost	MN VT

OTHER ISSUES

States are also grappling with other issues as part of basic reform packages or as incremental pieces designed to deal with specific problems in the system. These include:

- malpractice reform;
- increasing incentives for medical schools to provide primary care physicians, and for medical and nursing students to choose to practice in underserved areas of the state;
- encouragement of managed care approaches in the state; and
- Medicaid reforms to make the program more efficacious (such as the Oregon "mandating" model in which the state proposed prioritizing services based on their effects on patients' quality of life).

Some states have combined a number of approaches. For example, the 1992 Minnesota law setting up a Health Right program deals with a number of issues, including provision of subsidies for the uninsured, setting caps on the rate of growth of health programs, improving malpractice laws, reforming the insurance system, setting up a state office of rural health, and encouraging medical schools to provide more primary care physicians. The Minnesota program will be financed by taxes on providers and an increase in the cigarette tax.

CURRENT STATE OF AFFAIRS IN MICHIGAN

There have been many proposals to reform Michigan's health system over the past few years, but few have been adopted. One measure to address the shortage of health care professionals in rural areas was passed but has not been funded for the past two years.

The Senate-passed "Affordable Health Care Plan" encompassed thirty bills including creation of a low-cost basic health policy, income tax credits to encourage small employers and low-income workers to purchase insurance, physician discipline reforms, certificate of need reforms, and Good Samaritan protection for doctors and nurses providing emergency care in a hospital.

Legislation was introduced in 1993 to set up a single-payer system and a managed competition, regional approach to health care delivery. Malprctice reforms were also initiated. In 1993, several measures were considered to reform small group insurance, change licensure and discipline processes for health professionals, and extend health coverage of dependent children.

PRINCIPLES FOR LEGISLATORS INTERESTED IN STATE HEALTH REFORM

In light of the complexity of the issues and difficulties with achieving consensus, some guiding principles—gleaned from experiences in other states and political science research—might prove helpful.

1. LOOK AT THE "BIG PICTURE"

Health is a complex area with many actors—some portion of whom will oppose any reforms—and with many interrelationships.

In fact, health policy reform may be viewed as a mini-ecosystem in which change affecting one species or actor affects the well-being and survival of other actors. For example, reforms in the insurance market may lead to more companies deciding to "self-insure," and fee schedules may reduce quality, restrict access, or discourage development of better technology.

There is a tendency for all legislators to engage in "mole-bashing," the carnival game where the participant is given a hammer and asked to bash each mole that sequentially bounces up. The problem with mole-bashing, or dealing specifically with each problem that bounces up, is that another mole, or problem, will emerge that must be dealt with. Rather than a continual game of mole-bashing, legislative activity that encompasses a variety of interrelated areas, such as the Minnesota 1992 law, seems especially worthwhile.

2. STRIVE FOR MAJORITARIAN SUPPORT

Health is a salient issue that affects many people. Surveys have demonstrated time and time again that health is a major concern for the populace. For example, a recent Public Sector Consultants poll found that 69 percent of the Michigan respondents felt that the country was headed in the wrong direction in providing affordable health care. Other polls found that health was the number two issue on the public's mind during the 1992 national elections—behind only the economy in dominant issues.[6]

Business, labor, health providers, and federal and state officials agree. In a survey conducted by Lou Harris for the Metropolitan Life Insurance Company, only 12 percent of corporate executives, 14 percent of hospital CEOs, and none of the labor leaders polled felt that "on the whole, the health care system works pretty well and that only minor changes are necessary to make it work better."[7] Interestingly, the most sanguine group were physician leaders, some 31 percent of which agreed with the statement.

While such broad-based support might at first lead one to conclude that health reforms might be easy, we know that policies that benefit a large number of people but cost a small targeted group (called "entrepreneurial politics" by political scientist James Q. Wilson), are extremely contentious and difficult to enact.[8] Only with strong support from a diligent, dedicated entrepreneur or group that can convert a policy issue into a moralistic crusade can such policies hope to overcome opposition from the group or groups adversely affected. Support and conversion can come from health coalitions that have emerged in several states to help provide some focus for the views of "ordinary citizens." Coalitions in Washington, Maine and Massachusetts were active in pursuing health reform legislation in those states.

3. CONFRONT THE "VALUES" ISSUE UP FRONT

One of the issues raised by the recent attempt by Oregon to make tough choices about what services its Medicaid program would cover (while at the same time increasing the number of recipients eligible for Medicaid) was the necessity of making tough choices with some type of moral standard. What are the values of our society, reflected in our legislative decisions?

While few would argue that cost containment is unnecessary, getting rid of waste and efficiency in the system will solve only a small part of the problem. Further, one person's waste is another person's desperately needed (but perhaps only marginally beneficial) health care. Health care "waste" will have a name and a face attached to it, usually a desperate face. Another word for cost containment is rationing.

for example, women who have breast cancer that has failed to respond to all the standard therapies are doomed to die, unless they have access to an autologous bone marrow transplant. That procedure costs $150,000 per person and may offer only a 5 percent chance of three-year survival. Should the Medicaid program fund such last ditch medical interventions? How should just and caring and fiscally responsible state legislators respond to a request like that? Is this another instance of waste and inefficiency in our health care system that has a name like Susan or Sharon?

4. IDENTIFY A POLICY ENTREPRENEUR

One thread running through most case studies of successful state efforts at health care reform is the presence of a policy entrepreneur—a person well-placed in the political, bureaucratic (or sometimes academic) system who has the stature, power, and ability to persuade others and work hard to achieve this policy objective. The governor may be in a good position to do this, as well as legislative leadership, committee chairs, or others with standing and credibility. In several recent cases (Oregon and Vermont), that leadership was provided by a physician/politician or a physician/bureaucrat (Hawaii).

5. INCREMENTALISM IS NOT ALL BAD

While much of the work, and the examples cited here, highlighted states that have taken a more comprehensive approach, incremental reforms can be extremely valuable in fine-tuning approaches applicable to certain states or substate areas because they allow for experimentation and change based on lessons learned from small steps. Incremental reforms are also more politically appealing and, once established, can build a constituency that is supportive for further change. The comprehensive Hawaii system evolved from the original 1974 prepaid health care act, and Washington is building on a demonstration project to set up a public-private partnership to make low-cost health insurance eligible to those who need it. Connecticut's 1990 law expanding state-subsidized programs and instituting insurance market reforms was viewed as "a downpayment" on achieving universal access to health care by the Blue Ribbon Commission, which proposed it to the legislature. Florida law calling for basic health benefits for all Floridians sets up a series of deadlines for voluntary action. If these targets are not met by December 1994, an employer mandate will go into effect.

Perhaps the best example of incremental change has been in the Medicaid programs in Michigan and across the country. Many states have expanded Medicaid eligibility, covering pregnant women and children who would otherwise not qualify. Efforts to use managed care to improve both cost control and access have been initiated by a number of state Medicaid programs, including Michigan's. In addition, Michigan's Medicaid program has funded a series of demonstrations in an effort to foster innovation that might lead to improve service and lowered cost.

6. CONSIDER NEW "PROCESSES" FOR POLICY DEVELOPMENT

Over the past few years, a movement has been underway known as the Health Decisions movement. It refers to statewide, grass roots efforts to stimulate health policy discussions at the community level about difficult health decisions. As part of Oregon's rationing project, a number of community meetings were held throughout the state to help set priorities demanded by the program. Similarly, in Michigan, there is a project underway—Just Caring—that provides public forums where health care professionals and citizens engage in sustained and systematic discussion of critical moral issues in health.[9] Legislators should be aware of this effort and involved in it, drawing from the sessions clearer ideas of what the public needs and wants, and the priorities it chooses.

Another possibility in formulating policy that could also facilitate its enactment is use of a negotiation process, where parties representing a variety of interests come together and try to hammer out a policy they can agree on. The process has been used in writing regulations and in helping groups reach consensus on tough policy issues in health, education, and environment. Oregon has pursued a negotiated investment strategy in one key health area—programs for the elderly. Twice a year, the state's area agencies on aging, the state senior and disabled service division, providers, and advocacy groups meet to develop and implement programs targeted to the elderly.

7. LEARN FROM THE MISTAKES OF OTHERS

The Massachusetts program to provide universal health care is a good example of how a policy can go from a national model to a discredited disaster within a few short years—the victim of mounting health care costs and questionable political support.[10] Lessons learned from the repeal of catastrophic insurance at the national level are important too. Congress failed to tell the public clearly what the price of the program would be because its members were unable to face up to it politically. Additional problems were caused by the fact that many recipients were paying higher premiums for benefits they deemed not worthwhile (because most had obtained similar benefits from private policies). The lesson learned was not necessarily that the public is not willing to pay for services, but rather they are not willing to pay for services most do not want or need.

8. DO NOT ESTABLISH ANOTHER STUDY UNLESS YOU ARE WILLING TO ACT ON IT

States, including Michigan, often establish studies to issue recommendations for the state on key health care issues. While study commissions are clearly important, in the health area, commissions established with broad, general charges are often of little value. Rather, commissions designated to deal with specific problems, to choose among specific solutions, and with specific reporting targets seem most useful to state policymakers. For example, a 1992 Vermont law mandates a commission to make recommendations as to whether the state should adopt a single payor or all-payor model of health care.

9. DO NOT GIVE UP JUST BECAUSE THE ERISA REQUIREMENTS ARE STRICT AND MEDICAID WAIVERS ARE TIME-CONSUMING TO OBTAIN

While ERISA requirements limit some options available to states, many possible policies remain. Some states, such as Minnesota, are testing the reach of the ERISA provisions. Governors in several states are seeking exemptions from the law and lobbying for its revision. Bills have been introduced to revise the law to reduce its stranglehold on efforts to reform health insurance coverage. Recent media attention given to individuals who have seen dropped from (self-insured) group insurance plans and those unprotected by state insurance laws has raised the public visibility of ERISA's effect on health insurance.

The initial federal refusal to grant a Medicaid waiver for Oregon's rational care program was an apparent setback in the state's efforts to launch its innovative rationing program. However, President Clinton announced to the nation's governors early in his term that he intended to expedite the provision of waivers for both Medicaid and AFDC programs. The head of the General Accounting Office has urged the Congress to both amend the Medicaid waiver and offer a limited waiver of ERISA as a means of encouraging development of innovative state programs.

10. BE REALISTIC

Few proposals will solve all elements in need of reform. Further, some of the claims and demands of proponents are overstated. For example, some people rail about the excessive administrative costs of the current health care system and claim significant savings for some options, especially the single payor system. However, researchers who have studied administrative costs note that the costs may be overstated and that streamlining could come at the expense of other objectives, such as production of billing and clinical data used in the United States for medical education and for clinical and health services research. [11]

11. BE WARY OF THE SUBSTITUTION/COMPLEMENTARITY TRAP

Proponents and even policy analysts sometimes make assumptions that health programs will substitute, rather than complement, existing efforts. While clearly some programs will substitute for others in place, the likelihood is that new recipients will come "out of the woodwork" and that the costs will expand, rather than simply substitute for earlier expenditures. For example, programs providing home-health services for the elderly may not actually "save money" if they serve both those most-at-risk of nursing home placement and those who are simply old, but not likely candidates for publicly financed long-term care.

12. CONSIDER ADOPTION OF A "FAIL-SAFE" ON COSTS

Two states that have set in motion systems to provide direct subsidies to uninsured adults—Washington and Maine—have had to limit the program due to the costs. While at one point there were 22,000 enrolled in the Washington program, some 29,000 remained on a waiting list. Similarly, Maine's health care program targeted at adults not eligible for Medicaid has some 9,000 enrollees—out of an estimated 37,000 eligible.

13. DO SOMETHING

Rarely do policies burst full blown upon the system. Generally programs that passed in 1992 were also considered in 1991, 1990, and earlier. States innovative in health care reform, such as Hawaii, Oregon, Washington, and Massachusetts, have considered the issue for a long period of time and are often at first unsuccessful in reform efforts. They tend to build on the mistakes of the previous years to forge a program that best meets its needs.

WHY NOW?

Michigan legislators may well be wondering why they should act now. A newly elected president and a rejuvenated Congress made up of a majority of the president's party, may well gear up to respond to the public desire for change. Given a choice, the American people overwhelmingly choose the federal government to lead the charge in health care over states, with 62 percent choosing a federal lead; only 30 percent prefer states.[12]

WHY NOT WAIT FOR WASHINGTON TO ACT?

Several reasons for state action are key. First, states are one of the largest purchasers and providers of health services in the country. Thus states have a lot at stake in the decisions affecting the health care system. They are also primary regulators of health providers and have a major role in environmental and public health policy—areas likely to be affected by any national health care system. National law does not alleviate the need for Michigan law to deal with problems facing its health care system.

Second, if Congress and the president can agree on a proposal (a big *if*, even under a Democratic president and Congress), it will no doubt not solve all the problems. As discussed earlier, one proposal will not solve the complexity of the system, many policy strands must be put in place. Third, any national law will require state participation and cooperation. Fourth, development of federal law will be improved by inputs from the states, based on their experiences and responses to local problems and needs.

States want to be key players in any debate in health care—state, regional or national. But to do so, they must be clear about what their interests are and bring evidence for proposals that seem to work, based on state-level experience.

Finally, it is important to keep in mind that national health insurance has been on Washington's agenda for decades, with little to show for it. In spite of the apparent resurgence of interest in a comprehensive national health program, there is no certainty that it will come about. During the 1980s, the locus of health policymaking was "relocated" to state capitols. It may well stay there in the 1990s. Public opinion polls and national sentiment have failed to produce national health policy in recent years. As a historical reminder of the difficulty of predicting national action, one can cite the debate over the 1974 Hawaii Prepaid Health Care Act, in which the Chamber of Commerce opposed the bill, arguing that since a compulsory national health care law would soon preempt the state law, state law was unnecessary. [13]

Given Michigan's unenviable situation in which health care costs are growing at the national rate while per capita income is growing more slowly than the national rate, Michigan could easily reach a health care financing crisis before the nation as a whole is ready to act. Such a financial crisis could precipitate the bankruptcy of major health insurers, major urban hospitals, and many small rural hospitals, not to mention the teaching programs of the state's medical and nursing schools. The state might have to confront such a crisis on its own, with the rest of the nation trying to achieve a consensus on health system reform. Prudence would argue that the legislature undertake at least those reforms that would forestall such a financial crisis until the rest of the nation is ready for comprehensive reform.

NOTES

1. George Schieber, Jean-Pierre Poullier, and Leslie M. Greenwalk, "Health Care Systems in 24 Countries," *Health Affairs* 10 (1991): 22-38.
2. Paula A. Braveman et al., "Differences in Hospital Resource Allocation Among Sick Newborns According to Insurance Coverage," *Journal of the American Medical Association* 266 (1991): 3300-08.
3. Alice M. Rivlin, *Reviving the American Dream* (Washington D.C.: Brookings, 1992); Steffie Woolhandler and David U. Himmelstein, "The Deteriorating Administrative Efficiency of the U.S. Health Care System," *New England Journal of Medicine* 324 (1991): 1253-58.
4. Mark D. Smith et al., "Taking the Public's Pulse on Health System Reform," *Health Affairs* 11, no. 2 (1992): 125-33.
5. Marilyn Moon and John Holahan, "Can States Take the Lead in Health Care Reform?" *Journal of the American Medical Association.* 268, no.12 (1992): 1588-94.
6. Smith, et al. "Taking the Public's Pulse."
7. Metropolitan Life Insurance Company, *Trade-offs and Choices: Health Policy Options for the 1990s.* (New York: Metropolitan Life, 1992).
8. James Q. Wilson, *Bureaucracy: What Government Agencies Do and Why* (New York: Basic Books, 1991).
9. Leonard M. Fleck, "Just Caring Project. Information Packet," (East Lansing, MI: Center for Ethics, Michigan State University, 1992.
10. Camille Ascuaga, "Universal Health Care in Massachusetts: Lessons for the Future," *Health Policy Reform in America: Innovations from the States* (Armonk, N.Y.: M.E. Sharpe, 1992).
11. Kenneth E. Thorpe, "Inside the Black Box of Administrative Costs," *Health Affairs* 11, no. 2 (1992): 41-55.
12. Smith, et al. "Taking the Public's Pulse."
13. Deane Neubauer, "Hawaii: The Health State," *Health Policy Reform in America: Innovations from the States.* (Armonk, NY: M.E. Sharpe, 1992).

ADDITIONAL READINGS AND REFERENCES

Brown, Lawrence D. "Private-Public Solutions and Issues." *Inquiry* 29 (1992): 188-202.

Demitrack, Lucy B. "Governor Engler's 'New Priorities for a New Decade in Health Care.'" Lansing, MI: Michigan Public Health Association, 1992.

Fleck, Leonard M. "Just Health Care Rationing: A Democratic Decisionmaking Approach." *University of Pennsylvania Law Review* 140 (1992): 1597-1636.

General Accounting Office. *Access to Health Care: States Respond to the Growing Crisis* Washington D.C.: Government Printing Office, 1992

Goddeeris, John H. and Andrew J. Hogan, eds. *Improving Access to Health Care: What Can the States Do?* Kalamazoo, MI: W.E. Upjohn Institute for Employment Research, 1992.

Kronick, Richard. "Empowering the Demand Side: From Regulation to Purchasing." *Inquiry* 29 (1992): 213-31.

National Governors' Association. *A Healthy America: The Challenge for States*. Washington D.C.: NGA, 1992.

National Health Policy Forum. *Health Systems Reform, Then and Now :1970 and 1992*. Washington D.C.: National Health Policy Forum, 1992.

National Health Policy Forum. *The Role of Federal Standards in Health Systems Reform: How Much Leash Should ERISA Give the States?* Washington D.C.: National Health Policy Forum, 1992.

Weissert, Carol S. "Medicaid in the 1990s: Trends, Innovations, and the Future of the 'PAC-Man' of State Budgets." *Publius* 22 (1992): 93-109.

About the Contributors

RUTH BEIER

Ruth Beier is the Associate Director for Policy Analysis at Michigan State University's Institute for Public Policy and Social Research (IPPSR). The Policy Analysis Division of IPPSR houses the Michigan Database, the largest state and local database in the country. Analysts in the division use the database as well as their expertise in state and local applied economics to study public finance, state and local economic development, and other public policy issues. Before coming to Michigan State University, Ms. Beier served as Deputy Treasurer for the State of Michigan and as an economic analyst for Public Sector Consultants, Inc.

TIMOTHY BYNUM

Timothy Bynum is currently a Professor in the School of Criminal Justice and Associate Director of the Institute for Public Policy and Social Research at Michigan State University. He is an accomplished criminal justice researcher having directed a number of national and state-level research projects. In the recent past, he has directed a project funded by the Bureau of Justice Statistics, which investigated the variation in prison commitments in Michigan. He is currently finishing a project on the impact of race and gender on juvenile justice decisions. Dr. Bynum has published extensively from the results of his research, and has served as consultant to the U.S. Sentencing Commission, and as a reviewer of research proposals for the National Institute for Justice.

MARCUS CHEATHAM

Marcus Cheatham has a Master's Degree from the University of Oregon in International Studies. He will defend his Ph.D. dissertation in the summer of 1993. The title is "African Military Famines 1967-1991: The Political Economy of War and Hunger." He orginally trained in comparative politics, spending five years in Kenya where, among other things, he was an intern at the Institute for Development Studies at the University of Nairobi where he wrote a BA thesis on national language policy. At Michigan State University he specialized in methodology, working on a study of voting behavior in Zimbabwe, with Masipula Sithole, Chair of Political Science at the University of Zimbabwe; and on a survey of Zimbabwean farmers, with Mike Bratton.

BRUCE CHRISTENSON

Dr. Bruce Christenson is an Associate Research Scientist for American Institutes for Research (AIR) in Palo Alto, California. He is a former National Institute on Aging Post-doctoral fellow in Demography of Aging at the Population Studies Center of the University of Michigan, where work was begun on this report. He is working with Dr. Nan Johnson on an analysis of patterns of educational differences in current mortality in Michigan. Dr. Christenson's work at AIR also includes litigation support research in the area of employment discrimination.

JOEL CUTCHER-GERSHENFELD

Dr. Joel Cutcher-Gershenfeld is on the faculty at Michigan State University, with joint appointments in the School of Labor and Industrial Realtions and the Institute for Public Policy and Social Research. He is the coauthor (with Kevin Ford) of a forthcoming book on workplace training theory and policy. He is a coeditor (with Louis Ferman, Michele Hoyman and Ernie Savoie) of two additional books on training, one of which is focused on joint union-management training efforts, and the other on new directions in training practice. Dr. Cutcher-Gershenfeld is also coauthor (with Richard Walton and Robert McKersie) of two forthcoming books on negotiations. In addition, he is the author or coauthor of over thirty articles and book chapters on labor-management cooperation, dispute resolution, negotiations, new workplace systems, and other topics. Dr. Cutcher-Gershenfeld holds a Ph.D. in Industrial Relations from the Massachusetts Institute of Technology and a B.S. in Industrial and Labor Relations from Cornell University.

JOE T. DARDEN

Joe T. Darden received his Ph.D. in Urban Geography at the University of Pittsburgh in 1972. From 1971 to 1972, he was a Danforth Foundation Fellow at the University of Chicago. Dr. Darden received Michigan State University's Distinguished Faculty Award in 1984. He is currently Dean of Urban Affairs Programs and Professor of Geography at Michigan State University. His research interests are urban and social geography, with emphasis on minority groups. He is author of more than 100 publications. One of his most recent publications is a coauthored book entitled, *Detroit: Race and Uneven Development,* published by Temple University Press in 1987.

LEONARD M. FLECK

Dr. Leonard Fleck is currently (1985-) an Associate Professor in the Philosophy Department and in the Center for Ethics and Humanities in the Life Sciences at Michigan State University. Prior to that he taught for nine years in the Philosophy Department and School of Public and Environmental Affairs at Indiana University at South Bend. His main areas of teaching and research are medical ethics and health care policy. He has published over seventy articles in professional journals on topics in these areas. He is currently directing the statewide health reform project, "Just Caring: Conflicting Rights, Uncertain Responsibilities." He received his Ph.D. in Philosophy from St. Louis University in 1975. He is also the President of Medical Ethics Resource Network of Michigan.

J. KEVIN FORD

Dr. J. Kevin Ford is an Associate Professor of Industrial and Organizational Psychology at Michigan State University. Professor Ford's research interests include issues of workplace training design, evaluation, and transfer, as well as issues concerning the role of training within the strategic planning process of organizations. Kevin has authored over twenty articles and chapters and is on the editorial board of Personnel Psychology and the Journal of Training Research. In addition, Dr. Ford has consulted on training issues for several corporations, government agencies, and small businesses. Currently, he is conducting research for the Naval Training Systems Center that is focusing on improving the effectiveness of team training. He holds a Ph.D. in Psychology from Ohio State University and a B.S. in Psychology from the University of Maryland.

PHYLLIS T. H. GRUMMON

Dr. Grummon directs the Evaluation Unit in the Institute for Public Policy and Social Research at Michigan State University where she is an Assistant Professor. She also holds an adjunct appointment in the Educational Administration Department in the School of Education. Dr. Grummon has served on a number of national panels on assessment and was directly involved in assessment development when she worked for the State of Michigan. She has published a number of papers on assessment, particularly as it relates to the preparation of youth for the workforce.

LARRY HEMBROFF

Dr. Hembroff is a sociologist (Washington State, 1978) with expertise in survey research methods and social psychology. He has extensive experience with both the design and administration of computer assisted telephone interview (CATI) and mailed surveys. He oversees the ongoing research activities of IPPSR's Survey Research Division at all phases including sampling designs, training, questionnaire development, data collection, data processing and analysis. He has published articles in *Social Forces, The American Journal of Sociology, The Sociological Quarterly, Journal of Crime and Delinquency,* and *Social Psychology Quarterly.* He has also conducted numerous presidential polls, state and local policy surveys, program evaluation studies, community needs assessments, business needs assessments, and health-related surveys.

ANDREW J. HOGAN

Dr. Hogan has been an Associate Professor in the Office of Medical Education Research and Development, College of Human Medicine, Michigan State University since 1985. He also holds adjunct appointments in several departments and colleges at MSU. Dr. Hogan was the cofounder and is currently the acting Executive Director of the Michigan Health Benefits Network, a non-profit membership organization with fifty members, including private businesses, non-profit organizations, units of government, and labor union trusts. He also served as a member of the Academic Consortium of the Governor's Task Force on Access to Health Care, where he helped to draft the proposal for voluntary approaches to health care for the uninsured. His current research is on the cost of health services for HIV-infected individuals and effectiveness of cancer care. He is coeditor of the forthcoming monograph "Access to Health Care: What Can the States Do?" published by the W.E. Upjohn Institute for Employment Research.

NAN JOHNSON

Dr. Nan Johnson is Professor of Sociology at Michigan State University. Collaboratively with Dr. Christenson, her current work analyzes recent death certificate data on Michigan residents to find how educational patterns in mortality vary by age, sex, race, and selected causes of death. Additionally, as a half-time researcher for the Michigan Agricultural Experiment Station, she will study the association of metro/nonmetro residence with the death rates from these causes. In 1991, she was named a Fellow by the American Association for the Advancement of Science.

REX LAMORE

Rex LaMore is currently on assignment as the Program Leader for Community Development with the Michigan State University Cooperative Extension Service. He is also jointly appointed with the Department of Resource Development, where he teaches in Community and Economic Development, and the Office of the Vice-Provost for University Outreach. He is the founder and Project Leader for the Michigan Partnership for Economic Development Assistance, a U.S. Department of Commerce, Economic Development Administration University Research and Technical Assistance Center, concerned with economic development in distressed communities. Dr. LaMore received his B.S. and M.S. degrees at Michigan State University and his Ph.D. from the University of Michigan. With over fifteen years experience in community and economic development,

Dr. LaMore has focused his work on the unique challenges of revitalizing distressed communities.

BRENDAN MULLAN

Brendan Mullan is a demographer who teaches in the Department of Sociology and is a Research Associate with the Institute for Public Policy and Social Research at Michigan State University. He specializes in migration research and his current work focuses on processes of assimilation and adaptation among refugees in the United States and on the demography of rural populations. He is currently examining issues and problems confronting rural community leaders in Michigan.

KAREN ROBERTS

Karen Roberts is Assistant Professor in the School of Labor and Industrial Relations and Research Associate at the Institute for Public Policy and Social Research at Michigan State University. She is an active researcher and has published on a variety of issues related to workers' compensation, including benefit structures, access to benefits; why disputes arise, and the fairness of dispute resolution mechanisms, competitive pressures in insurance pricing; and international comparisons of programs as an indicator of the social contract. She has also consulted on workers' compensation issues in a variety of settings.

CAROL S. WEISSERT

Dr. Weissert is an Assistant Professor in the Department of Political Science at Michigan State University and a Research Associate for MSU's Institute for Public Policy and Social Research. She has a Master's in Public Administration from George Washington University and a doctorate in political science from the University of North Carolina at Chapel Hill. Her research focuses on national and state health policy issues, legislative behavior and intergovernmental relations. Recent work has appeared in *Legislative Studies Quarterly, American Politics Quarterly, Social Science Quarterly*, and *Publius*.

Index

A

Abortion: & legislative responsibility, 35-36; medicaid funding of, 32; Michigan residents' views on, 32-36, 47; rates of, *23*

Accident Fund of Michigan, the, 99, 106-7

Adult Alternative Training Fund, 77, *78*

Advanced Placement exams, 154-55

Affordable Health Care Plan, the, 190

African American population, 9, *15*, 16, 133; age composition of, 14-16; & AIDS, 63; & auto industry, 136; & educational access, 134, 139-41, 143-44; & housing access, 134, 137-39, 143, 145; infant mortality rate, 53-55; leading causes of death, 56-60, 62-63; life expectancy, 50-52, 55-61,62; mortality rate, 2, 49, 53-55, 68n.2; & unemployment, 135-37, 142

Age composition, Michigan, 8, 9-10, 13-14, 26

AIDS, 63

Alcohol tax. *See* Sin tax

All payor health care system, 186

Apprenticeship system, 84

Asian population, MI, 9

Assessment, educational: criticisms of, 152, 154; methods of, 152, 153-54; in Michigan, 155-57, 159, 161-62; vs. testing, 152, 153-54, 157

Assigned risk pool. *See* residual market

Auto industry, 41, 136

B

Baby boom generation, Michigan, 8, 9

Blanchard, James, 83, 137

Bureau of Workers' Disability Compensation, funding of, 110, 112

C

Cancer: & African American population, 56-60, 62, 63, 66-67; & Michigan mortality rate, 25; racial differences, 66-67